RETIREMENT ISSUES, PLANS AND LIFESTYLES

RETIREMENT SECURITY

NATIONAL AND INTERNATIONAL EFFORTS TO EXPAND COVERAGE

RETIREMENT ISSUES, PLANS AND LIFESTYLES

Additional books in this series can be found on Nova's website under the Series tab.

Additional e-books in this series can be found on Nova's website under the eBooks tab.

RETIREMENT ISSUES, PLANS AND LIFESTYLES

RETIREMENT SECURITY

NATIONAL AND INTERNATIONAL EFFORTS TO EXPAND COVERAGE

RAFAEL WILKINS
EDITOR

nova publishers
New York

Library of Congress Cataloging-in-Publication Data

ISBN: 978-1-63485-000-1

Published by Nova Science Publishers, Inc. † New York

CONTENTS

PREFACE

Millions of U.S. workers have little or no savings for retirement, potentially adding to future strains on state and national safety net programs. In addition to federal efforts, a growing number of states have proposed efforts to expand coverage in private sector workplace retirement savings programs. Other countries have also implemented similar efforts. This book examines recent estimates of coverage, including access and participation, as well as characteristics of workers who lack coverage; strategies used by states and other countries to expand coverage; and challenges states could face given existing federal law and regulations.

In: Retirement Security
Editor: Rafael Wilkins

ISBN: 978-1-63485-000-1

Chapter 1

Retirement Security: Federal Action Could Help State Efforts to Expand Private Sector Coverage*

United States Government Accountability Office

Why GAO Did This Study

Millions of U.S. workers have little or no savings for retirement, potentially adding to future strains on state and national safety net programs. In addition to federal efforts, a growing number of states have proposed efforts to expand coverage in private sector workplace retirement savings programs. Other countries have also implemented similar efforts. GAO was asked to study these state and international efforts.

GAO examined: (1) recent estimates of coverage, including access and participation, as well as characteristics of workers who lack coverage; (2) strategies used by states and other countries to expand coverage; and (3) challenges states could face given existing federal law and regulations. GAO primarily used SIPP data from 2012 (the most recent available). GAO also interviewed federal officials, national industry stakeholders, and officials and stakeholders in six states (California, Illinois, Maryland, Massachusetts, Washington, and West Virginia) and three countries (Canada, New Zealand,

* This is an edited, reformatted and augmented version of a United States Government Accountability Office publication, No. GAO-15-556, dated September 2015.

and the United Kingdom) selected based on the range of strategies used in efforts to increase coverage and recommendations from knowledgeable stakeholders.

WHAT GAO RECOMMENDS

GAO suggests that Congress consider providing states limited flexibility regarding ERISA preemption to expand private sector coverage. Agency actions should also be taken to address uncertainty created by existing regulations. Agencies generally agreed with GAO's recommendation. DOL plans to issue a proposed rule on state programs by the end of 2015.

WHAT GAO FOUND

About half of private sector workers in the United States—especially those who are low-income or employed by small firms—lack coverage from a workplace retirement savings program primarily because they do not have access. According to GAO's analysis of 2012 Survey of Income and Program Participation (SIPP) data, about 45 percent of private sector U.S. workers participated in a workplace retirement savings program—an estimate that is consistent with prior GAO work and other research. Using tax data to correct for under-reporting raised the share of workers participating to 54 percent, but still indicates many workers lack coverage. Among those not participating, the vast majority—84 percent—lacked access because they either worked for employers that did not offer programs or were not eligible for the programs that were offered, for example, because they were new employees or in specific jobs that were excluded from the program. In particular, lower-income workers and those employed by smaller firms were much less likely to have access to programs. However, among those who had access, the majority of these workers participated.

Key strategies to expand private sector coverage identified in the states and countries GAO reviewed include encouraging or requiring workplace access, automatic enrollment, financial incentives, and program simplification. For example, pending implementation, programs in two of the states GAO studied— California and Illinois—would require certain employers to automatically enroll workers in a state-run program, though workers could choose to opt-out. In the countries GAO studied, combining workplace access with automatic enrollment and financial incentives—tax preferences or employer contributions—has helped increase participation. Moreover, states and countries have tried to simplify program designs to (1) limit the responsibility and cost for employers and (2) reduce complexity, cost, and risk for workers. For example, some states intend to not only reduce burdens for employers by selecting and monitoring providers, but also reduce complexity for workers by limiting the number of investment options.

State and national stakeholders reported potential challenges with uncertainty created by the Employee Retirement Income Security Act of 1974 (ERISA) and agency regulations that could delay or deter state efforts to expand coverage. Generally, ERISA preempts, or invalidates, any state law relating to "employee benefit plans" for private sector workers, but different areas of uncertainty arise based on the details of each state effort. For example, four of the six states GAO reviewed intend to create payroll deduction individual retirement account (IRA) programs that would not be considered employee benefit plans. However, due to uncertainty created by ERISA, it is unclear whether a state can offer such programs or whether some of the program features would lead a court to find that they are, or relate to, employee benefit plans. Stakeholders also noted uncertainty caused by regulations from the Departments of Labor (DOL) and the Treasury meant to assist workers and employers. For example, DOL's regulation on payroll deduction IRAs was written before these state efforts were proposed and omits detail that, if included, could help reduce uncertainty. Given these uncertainties, states may face litigation and stakeholders noted that state programs could lose tax preferences if they were ruled preempted by ERISA.

ABBREVIATIONS

AGI	Adjusted gross income
CPS	Current Population Survey
DB	Defined benefit
DC	Defined contribution
DOL	Department of Labor
EBSA	Employee Benefits Security Administration
ERISA	Employee Retirement Income Security Act of 1974
IRA	Individual Retirement Account
IRC	Internal Revenue Code

MEP	Multiple Employer Plan
*my*RA	*My* Retirement Account
NEST	National Employment Savings Trust
PPA	Pension Protection Act of 2006
PRPP	Pooled Registered Pension Plans
SIMPLE	Savings Incentive Match Plan for Employees
SIPP	Survey of Income and Program Participation
SBA	Small Business Administration
SCF	Survey of Consumer Finances
SSA	Social Security Administration
Treasury	Department of the Treasury
U.K.	United Kingdom
VRSP	Voluntary Retirement Savings Plan

* * *

September 10, 2015

The Honorable Patty Murray
Ranking Member
Committee on Health, Education, Labor, and Pensions
United States Senate

Dear Senator Murray:

As workers live longer and face potential changes to future Social Security benefits, participating in a workplace retirement savings program is increasingly important to help ensure their retirement income security.[1] However, as we recently reported, 29 percent of households age 55 and older do not have any retirement savings or a defined benefit pension.[2] While some workers may choose not to participate in a workplace retirement savings program, a considerable number may not have the option either because their employer does not offer one or because the worker is not eligible to participate. Research has shown that other workers may not participate because of inertia—their employer's program requires workers to make an active decision to participate rather than automatically enrolling workers and allowing them to opt out. Although a growing number of employers have adopted automatic enrollment, a considerable number of programs still do not offer this feature and prior research shows that the overall coverage rate has not increased substantially.[3]

In response to the large share of the workforce that continues to lack coverage, there are mounting concerns that millions of workers will not have sufficient savings for retirement, adding to already significant burdens on state and national safety nets.[4] To address these issues, some federal and state legislators and the President have proposed efforts to expand workplace retirement savings program coverage in recent years. In addition, other countries face similar concerns and some have developed strategies to increase coverage that may offer lessons for the United States.

You asked us to review issues related to efforts to expand coverage in workplace retirement savings programs. This report examines:

1) recent estimates of workplace retirement savings program coverage, including eligibility and participation, and characteristics of workers who lack coverage;
2) strategies used by states and other countries to expand coverage among private sector workers; and
3) potential challenges states could face given existing federal law and regulations.

To develop estimates of retirement savings program coverage, we obtained data from the Survey of Income and Program Participation (SIPP) and output provided by the Census Bureau, which replicated our analysis using SIPP data linked to taxpayer data. In addition, we reviewed relevant literature and conducted interviews with experts and agency officials. We used data from the SIPP core survey and the topical module on retirement and pension coverage fielded from January to April 2012, the most recent data available. The survey collected data on about 52,000 individuals, including detailed information on work history, demographics, assets, and income. Using this data, we identified private sector workers, performed cross-tabulations, and developed an empirical model that included key demographic and occupational characteristics.[5] We examined the reliability of SIPP and Census data by interviewing the appropriate agency officials, reviewing documentation, and conducting selected data checks. Based on these assessments, we determined that the data were reliable for our purposes. (A more detailed description of our scope and methodology is provided in app. I.)

To identify strategies to expand private-sector workplace retirement savings program coverage and the potential challenges states could face given existing federal law and regulations, we obtained information about recent state efforts[6] and conducted case studies in six states—California, Illinois, Maryland, Massachusetts, Washington, and West Virginia. We selected these states, in part, to provide some parity based on the two broad categories of state efforts we identified—automatic IRA- and other voluntary account-type programs. As part of the case study reviews, we reviewed available documentation and interviewed industry representatives, state officials, and other stakeholders about advantages, disadvantages, and challenges of the strategies in selected state efforts. We also studied efforts to expand coverage in three countries that have voluntary workplace retirement savings programs—Canada, New Zealand, and the United Kingdom. We chose these countries based on their potential comparability to the United States. In addition, we examined one specific effort within the Australian superannuation program to address challenges specific to small businesses. As part of our review, we examined available documentation and analyzed the countries' systems based on strategies used to increase coverage and the potential effectiveness in the United States. We interviewed knowledgeable stakeholders and government officials from each country, as well as academics, about each strategy's strengths, weaknesses, tradeoffs, and applicability of lessons learned for the United States. We did not conduct an independent legal analysis to verify the information provided about the laws, regulations, or policies of the countries selected for this study, but rather relied on secondary sources and interviews with knowledgeable officials in each country.

We conducted this performance audit from June 2014 through September 2015 in accordance with generally accepted government auditing standards. Those standards require that we plan and perform the audit to obtain sufficient, appropriate evidence to provide a reasonable basis for our findings and conclusions based on our audit objectives. We believe that the evidence obtained provides a reasonable basis for our findings and conclusions based on our audit objectives.

BACKGROUND

Workers have a variety of options to save for retirement. While personal savings accounts and home equity can be used in retirement, many workers who save for retirement do so in tax-advantaged accounts available through their workplace. Their employers may sponsor an employee benefit plan, such as a 401(k) plan,[7] or make arrangements for employees to contribute to Individual Retirement Accounts (IRAs), such as payroll deduction IRAs, to help employees save for retirement.[8] (See table 1.)

Table 1. Description of Key Tax-Advantaged Workplace Retirement Savings Programs

Type of Tax-Advantaged Program	Description
Employee Benefit Plans	Employers can sponsor two broad types of retirement plans, referred to in the Employee Retirement Income Security Act of 1974 (ERISA) as pension plans: •Defined benefit (DB) plans, which promise a specified monthly benefit at retirement generally based on an employee's years of service and on salary, regardless of the performance of the plans' investments. •Defined contribution (DC) plans, in which benefits are based on contributions and the performance of the investments in participants' individual accounts. The dominant type of DC plan is a 401(k) plan but other types include 403(b) plans (for public education organizations, some non-profits employers, cooperative hospital service organization and self-employed ministers), and 457 plans (for governmental and certain non- governmental employers). In 2012, U.S. employers sponsored over 516,000 401(k) type plans providing access to more than 63 million workers with more than $3.5 trillion in plan assets.[a] Unlike DB plans, in which plan participants are eligible for a specific payment for life, 401(k) plan participants typically must make their own, sometimes complex, choices about their account balance both before and during retirement. For example, participants need to decide how much to contribute, how to invest, and how to spend down savings in retirement.

Table 1. (Continued)

Type of Tax-Advantaged Program	Description
Employer-provided IRAs	Employers can make arrangements for employees to contribute to IRAs to help them save for retirement. Two types of these IRAs are: •Payroll Deduction IRAs[b]: Through a payroll deduction IRA program, individuals may establish either traditional or Roth IRAs and make contributions by authorizing payroll deductions, which are forwarded by the employer to their IRAs.[c] If the employer is minimally involved as set out in Department of Labor (DOL) regulations, these programs are not considered pension plans under ERISA, and employers are not, therefore, plan fiduciaries. Traditional IRAs allow individuals to make contributions of earned income with taxes deferred on the contributions and the investment earnings until distributed at retirement. Once distributions are taken, they are generally taxed as ordinary income.[d] Roth IRAs, enacted as part of the Taxpayer Relief Act of 1997, allow eligible individuals to make nondeductible contributions and later receive tax-free distributions.[e] •Savings Incentive Match Plan for Employees (SIMPLE) IRAs: SIMPLE IRAs are a means by which employers with 100 or fewer employees can more easily provide a retirement savings program to their employees compared to providing a 401(k) or DB plan. Under such a program, eligible employees can direct a portion of their salary, within limits, to a SIMPLE IRA and employers must either (1) match the employees' contribution up to 3 percent of the employee's compensation[f] or (2) make nonelective contributions of 2 percent of each employee's salary for all employees making at least $5,000 for the year.[g]

Type of Tax-Advantaged Program	Description
	The employee salary reduction contribution limit for 2015 is $12,500. Employers can elect to permit catch-up contributions for those at least age 50, which in 2015 are limited to $3,000.[h]

Source: GAO review of select laws and regulations. | GAO-15-556

[a] U.S. Department of Labor, Employee Benefits Security Administration, Private Pension Plan Bulletin: Abstract of 2012 Form 5500 Annual Reports, Version 1.2 (Washington, D.C.: January 2015).

[b] For more information see GAO, *Private Pensions: Better Agency Coordination Could Help Small Employers Address Challenges to Plan Sponsorship*, GAO-12-326 (Washington, D.C.: March 5, 2012) and GAO, *Individual Retirement Accounts: Government Actions Could Encourage More Employers to Offer IRAs to Employees*, GAO-08-590 (Washington, D.C.: June 4, 2008).

[c] The dollar limit on all IRA contributions is adjusted annually for cost-of-living increases. 26 U.S.C. §§ 408(o)(2), 408A(c)(2) and 219(b)(5). For 2015, the combined maximum contribution for all traditional and Roth IRAs in total is $5,500. Individuals age 50 and older are eligible to make additional catch-up contributions of $1,000. 26 U.S.C. § 219(b)(5)(B). Taxpayers age 701/2 and older can contribute to a Roth IRA only. 26 U.S.C. §§ 219(d)(1) and 408A(c)(4). Any contribution exceeding the annual limit or made by an ineligible taxpayer is subject to a 6 percent excise tax on the amount of excess contributions. 26 U.S.C. § 4973(a).

[d] 29 U.S.C. § 408.

[e] 29 U.S.C. § 408A.

[f] 26 U.S.C. § 408(p)(2)(A)(iii) and (C)(ii).

[g] 26 U.S.C. § 408(p)(2)(B)(i). For employees who participate in other employer plans during the year, the overall total salary reduction contribution limit for all plans is $18,000 in 2015.

[h] 26 U.S.C. § 414(v)(2)(B)(ii) and (C).

Workers may also choose to save on their own in an IRA to increase their retirement savings. However, our recent work shows that approximately 95 percent of money contributed to traditional IRAs in 2008 was from rollovers, primarily from employee benefit plans.[9]

Despite the various options available for employers to offer a workplace retirement savings program, our prior work and other research shows a persistent gap in coverage among private sector workers.[10] While estimates of participation rates can vary depending on the nature of the study sample (e.g., whether it includes full and part-time workers or is based on household or firm-level data), research consistently indicates that many workers do not participate in a workplace retirement savings program. For example, one study using household data from the Current Population Survey (CPS) shows that the participation rate of private sector workers has declined slightly from about half of full- and part-time workers in the late 1990s to 43 percent in 2012.[11] Similarly, another study using CPS data found that the participation rate among private sector workers ages 21 to 64 has fluctuated over the time period from 2000 to 2012 from a high of about 47 percent in 2000 to a low of about 39 percent in 2012.[12] In addition, a study using firm-level data from the 2014 National Compensation Survey reports that 48 percent of private sector workers participate in a retirement plan.[13]

Efforts to Expand Workplace Retirement Savings Program Coverage in the United States

The President and some members of Congress have proposed various efforts over the years to expand workplace retirement savings program coverage among private sector workers.[14] These efforts generally strive to overcome obstacles for employers to offer workplace retirement savings programs or for workers to participate. In particular, our prior research found that small employers may be reluctant to offer these programs because of administrative burden and potential fiduciary risk.[15] Some workers, on the other hand, may lack the financial literacy or resources to participate.

Automatic Enrollment

To foster retirement saving among the portion of the workforce who have been offered an employee benefit plan but do not participate, some employers have adopted automatic enrollment policies for their defined contribution plans.[16] Under automatic enrollment, eligible workers are enrolled into the plan, unless they explicitly choose to opt out, as opposed to the more traditional method in which workers must take action to join a plan. Employers who have adopted automatic enrollment must also establish default contribution rates and default investment vehicles for workers who do not specify these choices.[17] Employers may also adopt automatic escalation policies, which increase contribution rates on a predetermined schedule—even without active decisions by employees— typically up to a pre-defined maximum contribution rate. The Internal Revenue Code (IRC) and the

Employee Retirement Income Security Act of 1974 (ERISA) were amended by the Pension Protection Act of 2006 (PPA) to facilitate the use of automatic enrollment, and Department of Labor (DOL) and the Department of the Treasury (Treasury) promulgated implementing regulations.[18]

Saver's Credit

To encourage low- and middle-income individuals and families to save for retirement, the IRC was amended by the Economic Growth and Tax Relief Reconciliation Act of 2001 to allow a credit against federal income taxes of up to $2,000 for qualified retirement savings.[19] Eligibility for the Saver's Credit is based on workers' adjusted gross income (AGI) and contributions to employee benefit plans and IRAs with the credit phasing out at certain income limits, depending on the size of the household. Since the adoption of the Saver's Credit, bills have been introduced to further encourage low-income workers to save for retirement, including making the tax credit refundable and increasing the rate of the tax credit for retirement contributions.

myRA

In January 2014, the President directed Treasury to create the *My* Retirement Account (*my*RA) program, a new retirement savings account for Americans looking for a simple, safe, and affordable way to start saving. Individuals who voluntarily open *my*RA accounts will be able to set up recurring payroll deduction contributions that will be invested in nonmarketable retirement savings bonds only available to participants in the program.[20] The savings bond is backed by the Treasury, will not go down in value, and will earn interest equal to the rate of return provided in a fund offered in the federal employee retirement plan.[21] The retirement savings bonds will mature at the earlier of 30 years from the date the bond is first issued or when the total value of the bond reaches $15,000. At that time balances will be transferred to a private-sector Roth IRA.[22] Participants are not charged fees for *my*RA accounts—administrative costs are paid by the Treasury. *my*RA accounts follow Roth IRA rules, so contributions are made with after-tax income but may be withdrawn tax-free at any time. Moreover, not all Americans will be eligible to participate due to IRA contribution limits based on modified adjusted gross income.[23] Unlike some commercial IRA accounts, *my*RA does not impose minimum balance or minimum contribution requirements—individuals will be able to open accounts with no start-up cost and can choose to automatically contribute any amount each payday.

Legislative Proposals

Members of Congress have also introduced bills over the years to foster retirement savings among those who work for employers that do not sponsor employee benefit plans. One group of proposals would establish "automatic IRAs" for workers not covered by an employee benefit plan.[24]

Under an automatic IRA, employers would be required to make available an arrangement in which employees would be automatically enrolled and contributions would be made through automatic payroll deduction, with an opt-out provision for participants.[25] In addition, some bills would allow for more widespread adoption of multiple employer plans by enabling employers without a common interest to sponsor such plans.[26] Appendix III provides a description of the bills we identified.

Federal Regulation of Employee Benefit Plans and Individual Retirement Accounts

In the United States, employers are generally not required to provide employee benefit plans, including pension plans, to any employees. When they do, however, employee benefit plans are generally regulated at the federal level, providing employers with largely uniform nationwide standards.[27] Most significantly, plans are subject to the requirements of ERISA, which are generally enforced by DOL's Employee Benefits Security Administration (EBSA) and various provisions of the Internal Revenue Code (IRC), which is enforced by the Internal Revenue Service (IRS).[28] ERISA was enacted to, among other things, protect the interests of plan participants and their beneficiaries and set minimum standards for most private sector pension plans, including rules for fiduciary conduct and prohibited transactions.[29] The IRC and ERISA define prohibited transactions and list exemptions to them.[30] In addition DOL may grant exemptions.[31] To carry out its responsibilities under ERISA, EBSA promulgates regulations and issues various forms of guidance. The IRS is primarily responsible for ensuring that plans meet certain requirements for tax-favored treatment.[32]

ERISA and relevant provisions of the IRC establish minimum requirements and standards for private-sector employee benefit plans. ERISA establishes minimum participation, vesting, and funding standards for plans.[33] For example, ERISA limits the age and the length-of-service that employers can require employees to meet to be eligible for a plan. To qualify for tax benefits under IRC, plans must also meet minimum participation, vesting, and funding standards.[34] An employer may also establish a plan that excludes certain groups of employees as long as the ERISA and IRC requirements are met.[35] For example, an employer may establish and maintain a plan that excludes workers in certain job categories or geographic locations.[36]

Lastly, IRS is responsible for enforcing IRA tax requirements but IRS and DOL share responsibility for overseeing prohibited transactions relating to IRAs that are not ERISA-covered plans.

ERISA Preemption

ERISA includes a provision stating that ERISA supersedes any and all state laws as they "relate to" any employee benefit plan covered under ERISA.[37] This ERISA preemption provision has a relatively small number of exceptions[38] and reflects a policy judgment that nationwide uniformity respecting employee benefit plans outweighs the value of state differentiation. In addition to statutory provisions, "state laws" encompasses decisions, rules, regulations, and any other state action having the effect of law.[39]

Based on statutory interpretation and its review of the legislative history of ERISA, in 1983 the Supreme Court held that a state law "relates to" an employee benefit plan and is preempted "if it has a connection with or reference to such a plan."[40] The Court has emphasized that state law may be preempted even if not specifically designed to affect such plans.[41] Furthermore, even if a state law is not in conflict with ERISA but is, in fact, consistent with it because, for example, it promotes retirement security, it is not spared from ERISA preemption if it "relates to" an employee benefit plan.[42] The broad scope of ERISA's preemption provision has permitted large employers to provide pension plans to their employees without having to establish multiple plans or plan policies depending on differing requirements from state to state. In addition, ERISA's preemption provision helps to ensure that participants are protected by several safeguards. For example, ERISA establishes minimum participation and vesting standards, imposes fiduciary duties on plan sponsors, and authorizes DOL to enforce its requirements.

A 1995 Supreme Court case, however, raised some question regarding the Court's prior attempts to construe "relate to" and the expansiveness of ERISA. Furthermore, in 2010 a federal appeals court appeared to limit the scope of ERISA preemption when it upheld a local law requiring, among other things, that covered employers make a certain level of health care expenditures[43] on behalf of their employees.[44]

Gaps in Access Leave Many Low-Income and Other Workers without Workplace Retirement Savings Program Coverage

About half of private sector workers did not participate in a workplace retirement savings program in 2012. While some workers chose not to participate, we found that most workers who did not have coverage lacked access to such programs.[45] Among those not participating, the majority worked for an employer that did not offer a program or they were not eligible for the programs that were offered. In particular, lower income workers and those employed by smaller firms were much less likely to have access to programs, after controlling for other factors. In addition to lacking access, certain workers, such as lower income, service sector, and younger workers, were also less likely to participate in programs even when provided access. However, the majority of these workers participated when they had workplace access.

Lack of Coverage Is Driven by Gaps in Access

Roughly half of private sector workers participate in a workplace retirement savings program, according to 2012 data. Specifically, self-reported SIPP data indicate that 45 percent of all private sector workers were participating in a program.[46] However, prior research using SIPP data linked with W-2 tax records has shown that some individuals under- report their participation.[47] To address this issue, we examined similarly linked data to correct for under-reporting and the resulting participation rate increased to 54 percent (see fig. 1).[48] While the W-2 adjusted data show a moderate increase in participation, both measures indicate that many workers lack coverage in a workplace retirement program.[49] Our findings are similar to estimates from our prior work and other studies.[50] For example, the prior research that linked 2006 SIPP data with W-2 tax records shows, using this approach, that the measure of participation among private sector workers increased from 45 percent to 58 percent.[51] A more recent update to this study found that participation further increased to 62 percent in 2012, although the age range of this study differed from our work—this study examined private sector workers ages 21 to 64, while we focused on private sector workers ages 18 and over.[52] Other more recent data from the 2014 National Compensation Survey, a firm level survey conducted by the Bureau of Labor Statistics, show that 48 percent of private sector workers participated in a retirement plan.[53]

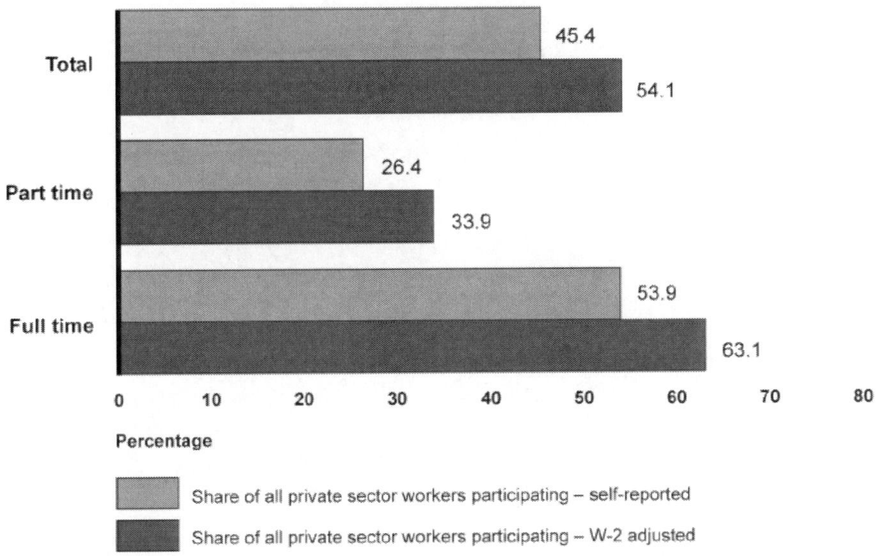

Source: GAO analysis of 2012 data from the Survey of Income and Program Participation and the U.S. Census Bureau. | GAO-15-556.

Figure 1. Share of Private Sector Workers Participating in a Workplace Retirement Savings Program, 2012.

Among workers who are not participating, we found that the gap in coverage is mainly due to a lack of access rather than a failure to participate. The vast majority of workers who do not participate–84 percent—reported they did not have access to a workplace retirement program. Access depends on two essential factors: (1) The employer must offer a program, and (2) the worker must be eligible to participate (see fig. 2).[54]

Of these two factors, we found that the lack of access was primarily due to employers not offering a retirement program. Specifically, among those who do not participate, 68 percent reported they worked for an employer that did not offer a program, and another 16 percent reported they were not eligible for the program their employer offered (see fig. 3).[55] Only 16 percent of those who did not participate reported being eligible and not participating.

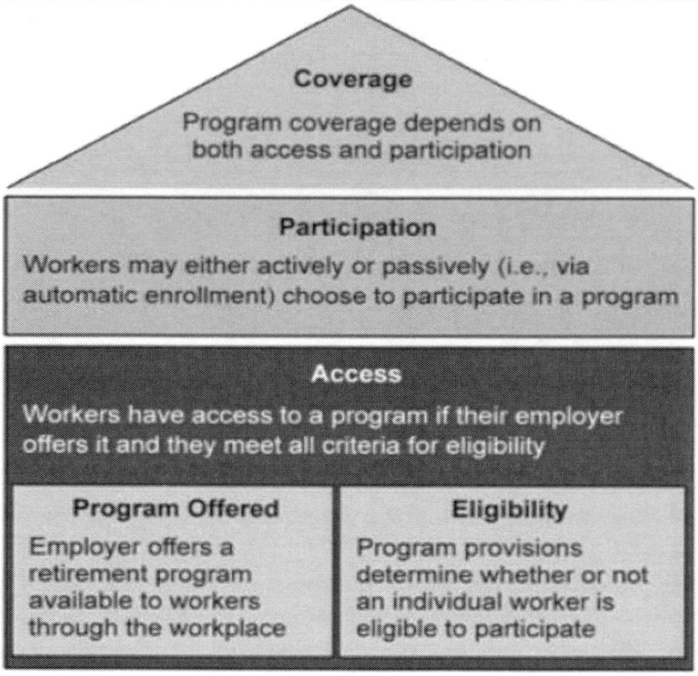

Source: GAO analysis. | GAO-15-556.

Figure 2. Building Blocks of Workplace Retirement Savings Program Coverage.

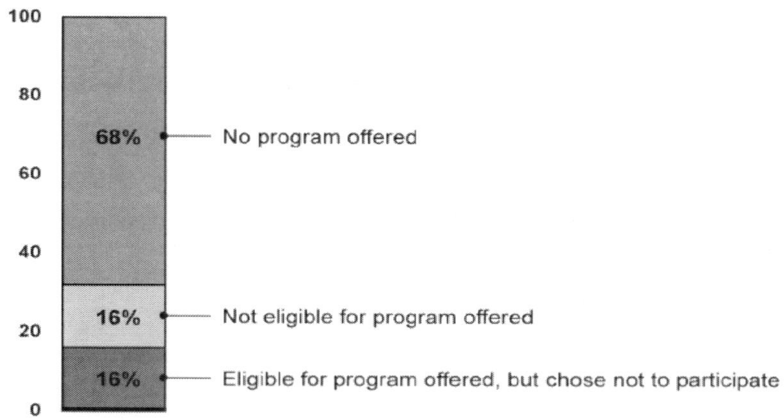

Source: GAO analysis of 2012 data from the Survey of Income and Program Participation. | GAO-15-556.

Figure 3. Percentages of Private Sector Workers Not Participating in a Workplace Retirement Savings Program by Reason Given, 2012.

Lower Income Workers and Those Employed by Smaller Firms Are Much Less Likely to Have Coverage

Certain types of workers, such as those with lower incomes, are much less likely to have coverage compared to other workers. Lower-income workers, in particular, are much less likely to have access to workplace retirement programs and to choose to participate when programs are available. Compared to workers in the lowest income quartile, our analysis found workers in the highest income quartile were nearly 4 times as likely to work for an employer that offers a program, after controlling for other factors.[56] The gap in access exists across the income distribution and is even larger when it comes to eligibility—workers in the third and fourth quartiles were, respectively, 4.4 and 7.5 times as likely to be eligible for a program offered by their employer than workers in the lowest income quartile. In addition, lower-income workers had a lower likelihood of participating even when they were eligible (see fig. 4).[57]

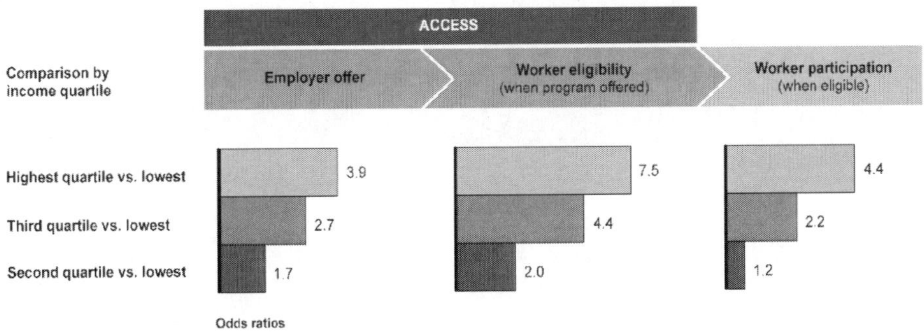

Source: GAO analysis of 2012 data from the Survey of Income and Program Participation. | GAO-15-556.

Note: This figure shows the difference in the likelihood, or odds, of the following outcomes by income quartile, after controlling for other factors: 1) having an employer that offers a retirement program, 2) being eligible (among those offered a program), and 3) participating in a program (among those who are eligible). We used separate regressions to estimate these likelihoods to compare the size of the effects of various factors at each stage. Odds ratios are plotted on a multiplicative, rather than additive, scale.

Figure 4. Effect of Income on Likelihood of Workplace Retirement Savings Program Coverage after Controlling for Other Factors.

The combined effects of lower access and lower participation result in large gaps in coverage across income groups (see fig. 5). Overall, approximately 14 percent of workers in the lowest income quartile participated in a program compared to 57 percent and 76 percent of those in the third and fourth income quartiles, respectively. Similarly, according to the W-2 adjusted data, 22 percent of workers in the lowest income quartile participated in a program compared to 67 percent and 84 percent of those in the third and fourth income quartiles.

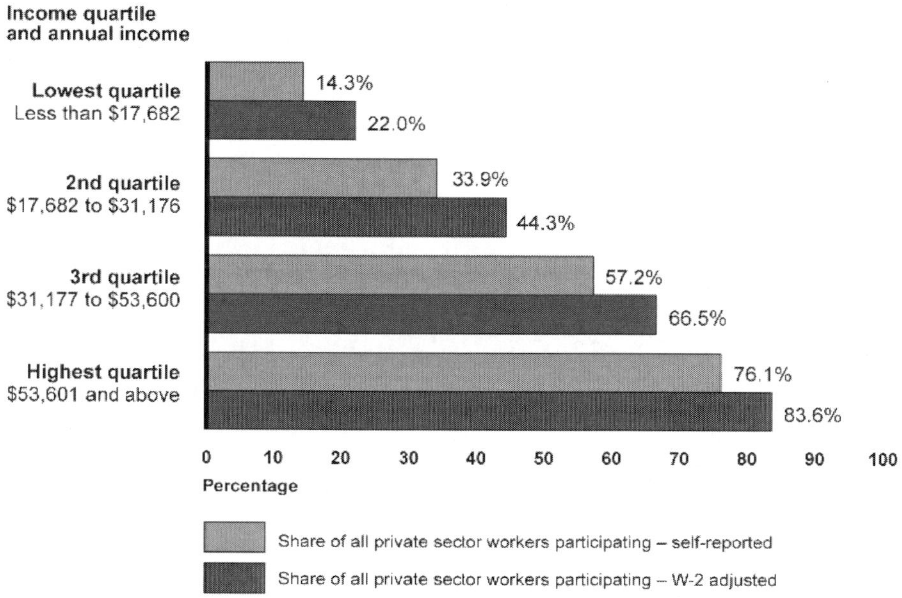

Source: GAO analysis of 2012 data from the Survey of Income and Program Participation and the U.S. Census Bureau. | GAO-15-556.

Note: Each income quartile represents about 25.5 million private sector workers.

Figure 5. Share of Private Sector Workers Participating in a Workplace Retirement Savings Program by Income Quartile, 2012.

In addition to income, working for a small or mid-size firm is one of the most important factors associated with a lack of coverage. In particular, workers at smaller firms were much less likely to have coverage than workers at larger firms because their employer did not offer a program. Workers at the largest firms were more than 9 times as likely to have an employer that offered a program compared to those who worked for firms with 50 or fewer workers, after controlling for other factors. Even outside the smallest firms, the difference in the likelihood of an employer offering a program was considerable when comparing mid-size and larger firms (see fig. 6). As we have previously reported, smaller firms face challenges in offering programs, such as the perceived complexity and risk of establishing and administering a program.[58] Moreover, smaller and newly formed firms have higher rates of "churn"—business formation and dissolution—and are less likely to offer a program initially. Certain characteristics associated with small employers may also contribute to the challenges of starting and maintaining a program. For example, small employers are more likely to encounter higher rates of worker turnover. In addition, small employers' operating revenue can be uncertain from year to year.

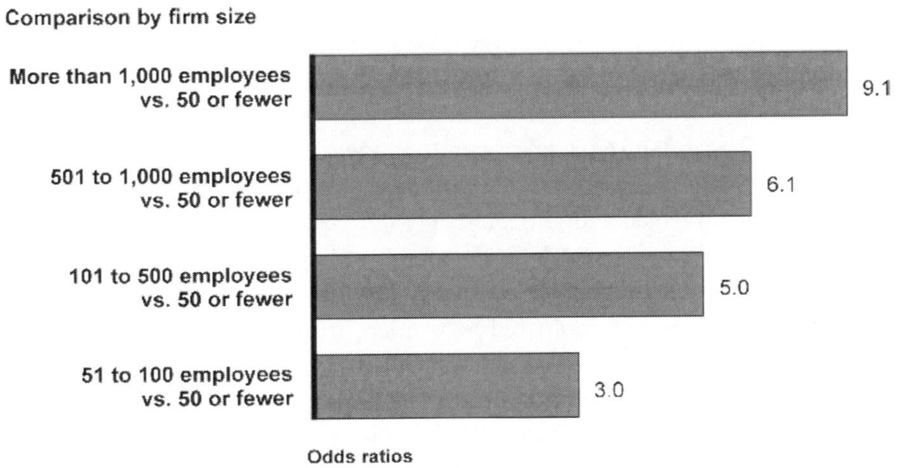

Source: GAO analysis of 2012 data from the Survey of Income and Program Participation. | GAO-15-556.

Note: Odds ratios are plotted on a multiplicative, rather than additive, scale.

Figure 6. Effect of Firm Size on Likelihood of Employer Offering a Workplace Retirement Savings Program after Controlling for Other Factors.

Outside of whether an employer offers a program, firm size had little to no effect on eligibility or participation. Workers at small or mid-size firms that offer a program were just as likely to be eligible as workers at larger firms with up to 1,000 workers, after controlling for other factors. And workers at the largest firms—more than 1,000 workers—were only slightly more likely than workers at the smallest firms—50 or fewer workers—to be eligible. Similarly, among those who were eligible, workers at the largest firms were only slightly more likely to participate compared to workers at the smallest firms, although this effect was only statistically significant using the W-2 adjusted data.[59] Overall, about 23 percent of workers at firms with 50 or fewer workers participated in a program compared to 60 percent of workers at firms with more than 1,000 workers. Corresponding participation rates from the W-2 adjusted data were 31 percent and 68 percent, respectively.

In addition to income and firm size, other characteristics were also significantly associated with whether a worker has coverage, after controlling for other factors. For example:

- **Part-time:** Part-time workers were less likely to have coverage, primarily due to a lack of access. Specifically, compared to part-time workers, full-time workers were about 2.6 times more likely to be eligible for a program offered by their employer. Full-time workers were also more likely to work for an employer that offers a program, but the difference in likelihood was considerably smaller—by a factor of 1.2. Among those who were eligible, full-time workers were only slightly more likely to participate than part-time workers; however this result was not significant using the W-2 adjusted data.[60]
- **Occupation:** Workers in management, business, science, and arts occupations were nearly twice as likely to work for an employer that offers a program compared to workers in service occupations. Those in service sector occupations were also less likely to participate in programs when they had access.[61] However, occupation was not associated with whether workers were eligible for programs offered by their employers.
- **Age:** Compared to older workers, younger workers were generally less likely to be eligible for a program and to participate when eligible.

For example, among those eligible, workers ages 18 to 24 were roughly one-half as likely to participate as workers ages 25 to 34.[62] This pattern holds when comparing progressively older age categories of workers with younger workers, with the exception of workers ages 65 and older. Workers ages 65 and older were less likely to have access to a program compared to workers ages 25 to 34, but were no less likely to participate if they were eligible.

Given Access, Most Workers Participate

Among workers who are least likely to participate—such as lower income, service sector, and younger workers—the majority did so when they had workplace access. The share of workers in the lowest and 2nd income quartiles who participated when eligible was 63 percent and 74 percent, respectively (see fig. 7). Corresponding figures from the W-2 adjusted data were 68 percent and 79 percent. Similarly, the participation rate for eligible service sector workers was 70 percent (74 percent according to W-2 adjusted data). Among the categories of workers we examined, the lowest participation rate among eligible workers was for those ages 18 to 24, but still more than half, 54 percent, participated (59 percent according to W-2 adjusted data).

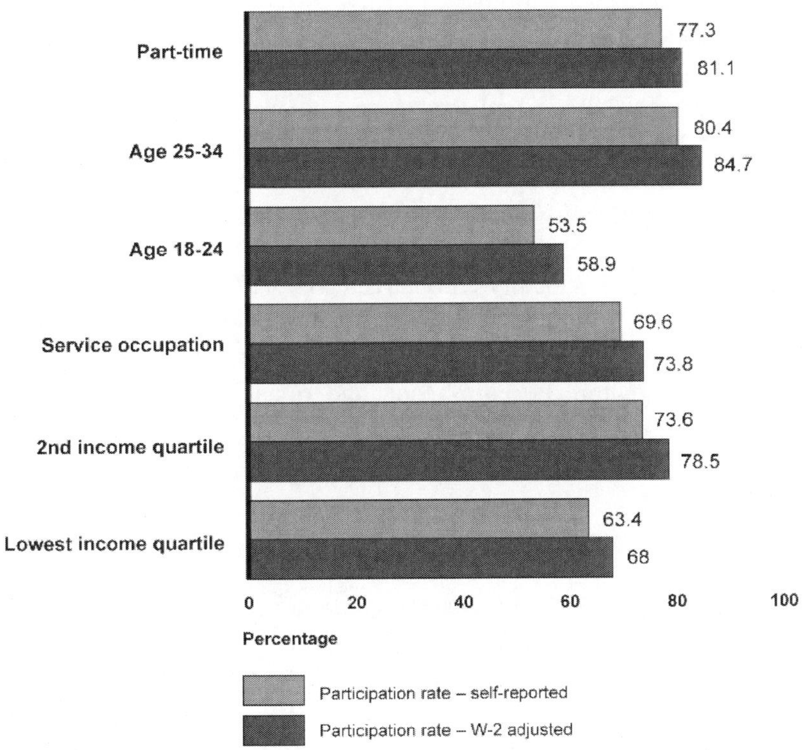

Source: GAO analysis of 2012 data from the Survey of Income and Program Participation and the U.S. Census Bureau. | GAO-15-556.

Figure 7. Participation Rate in Workplace Retirement Savings Programs among Eligible Workers by Various Characteristics, 2012.

STATES AND OTHER COUNTRIES USE SIMILAR KEY STRATEGIES TO EXPAND RETIREMENT COVERAGE

States and Countries We Reviewed Often Combine Workplace Access, Automatic Enrollment, and Financial Incentives

In the six states we studied, proposals were made and, in some, laws enacted in an effort to expand coverage that would combine workplace access to a retirement savings program with automatic enrollment and financial incentives[63] —an approach that has helped increase worker participation in countries we studied.[64] For example, the United Kingdom (U.K.) implemented reforms that require private sector employers to automatically enroll eligible workers in a workplace retirement savings program, allowing workers to contribute to individual accounts and receive financial incentives in the form of employer contributions and tax preferences.[65] A government study published in March 2015 found that since implementation of these reforms began in October 2012, various stakeholders generally perceived them as successful to date by bringing millions of new people into retirement savings programs, with significantly fewer individuals opting out than predicted.[66] In fact, the government reported that by the end of 2014 more than 5 million workers had been automatically enrolled and only 12 percent of workers had opted out in 2014.[67] Similar to the U.K. and other countries, state efforts[68] we reviewed in the United States would use a range of approaches to combine workplace access, automatic enrollment, and financial incentives to expand coverage.

Workplace Access

The six state efforts we reviewed would expand workplace access for uncovered workers in two ways. Some of the states are *encouraging* small employers to offer workplace access by creating state-run programs or state-facilitated marketplaces by which employers can voluntarily offer workers access to a retirement savings program and payroll deduction. For example, Massachusetts is developing a state-run 401(k) plan[69] that not-for-profit employers with fewer than 20 employees in the state can adopt. Similarly, Washington plans to create a state-facilitated marketplace that would list a variety of qualified providers from which employers with fewer than 100 employees could choose to offer their workers. Laws or bills in other states, such as California, Illinois, and Maryland, would *require* employers with more than a certain number of employees, and which do not already offer an employee benefit plan to make their payroll systems available for workers to contribute via payroll deduction.[70] To ensure these employers are able to find a reasonable option to meet this requirement, these states would create state-run programs. (See table 2.)

State stakeholders told us that state efforts to expand coverage in workplace retirement savings programs were designed to provide workplace access because research and experience by employee benefit plans in the United States has shown that workers are more likely to save for retirement if their employer offers a retirement savings program.[71] DOL and the Small Business Administration (SBA) note that payroll deduction—an amount of salary taken from a worker's paychecks— allows workers to save smaller amounts each pay period instead of waiting until the end of the year to set aside money in an IRA. And a study prepared for SBA concluded that the biggest step small employers could take to increase worker retirement savings was to offer them access to a plan.[72] Workplace access enables workers to take advantage of payroll deduction for retirement savings. Federal and state officials and state stakeholders noted that using payroll deductions makes contributing easy for most workers, helping them develop a habit of saving.

The countries we reviewed have also taken steps to encourage or require employers to provide workplace access for uncovered workers that use similar approaches as state efforts (see fig. 8). As part of the U.K.'s effort, the government created the National Employment Savings Trust (NEST) to provide employers with a reasonable option to meet the requirement to provide workers access. This approach is similar to efforts in California, Illinois, and Maryland, and to some state efforts without an employer requirement that still create a state-run program, such as Massachusetts and West Virginia.[73] In addition, New Zealand and Canada would encourage or require certain employers to offer workplace access.[74]

Instead of creating a state-run program for employers, though, New Zealand and Canada license service providers to offer programs that meet established criteria—an approach similar to the marketplace in Washington State.

Table 2. Summary of Efforts to Expand Workplace Retirement Savings Program Coverage for Private Sector Workers in Selected States

	California	Illinois	Massachusetts	Maryland	Washington	West Virginia
Recent approach	State-run program	State-run program	State-run program	State-run program	State-facilitated marketplace	State-run program
Status[a]	Enacted, conducting feasibility study[b]	Enacted, developing implementation[c]	Enacted, developing implementation	Not enacted	Enacted	Not enacted
Savings vehicle[d]	Payroll deduction IRA	Payroll deduction IRA	Employee benefit plan (401(k) plan)	Payroll deduction IRA for worker contributions Employee benefit plan (profit sharing) for employer contributions	Payroll deduction IRA and SIMPLE IRA[e]	Employee benefit plan or IRA
Target employer size	Employers with **5 or more** employees	Employers with **25 or more** employees	Not-for-profit employers with **not more than 20** employees	Employers with **5 or more** employees	Employers with **fewer than 100** employees[f]	Employers with **no more than 100** employees
Employer participation	Certain employers are **required** to automatically enroll eligible employees[g]	Certain employers are **required** to automatically enroll eligible employees	Voluntary	Certain employers are **required** to automatically enroll eligible employees	Voluntary	Voluntary
If required, exempted employers	Employers that already offer a qualified plan or automatic enrollment payroll deduction IRA	Employers in business for 2 years or less, or that already offer any qualified plan	N/A	Employers in business for 2 years or less, or that already offer an employer sponsored plan[h]	N/A	N/A

Source: GAO analysis of state laws and bills, and testimonial information from knowledgeable industry representatives. | GAO-15-556.

Note: We selected these six states for case studies because they were identified as having “leading” state efforts by relevant government officials and knowledgeable industry representatives. For states that have enacted laws, we have included a description of that enacted law in this table. For the two states that have not enacted legislation, Maryland and West Virginia, we described each state’s most recent substantive legislative effort that we identified. In recent years, all six states may have attempted a variety of efforts to expand retirement savings coverage (see app. IV).

[a] While some states have enacted legislation, none have fully implemented programs. As described later in this report, implementation of these efforts is contingent on their legal feasibility.

[b] In addition to requiring a feasibility study, California law requires enactment of a subsequent authorizing statute that expresses approval for the program to be fully implemented before the program may be opened for enrollment.

[c] The Illinois law also prohibits implementation of the program if the IRA arrangements offered under it fail to qualify for the preferential tax treatment afforded IRAs.

[d] We characterized the savings vehicles for each state as they are characterized in the laws or bills involved. We note, however, that ERISA provides that only employers may establish or maintain pension plans and some federal courts have read this to mean that the entity that maintains a plan and plan participants must be tied by a common economic or representational interest, unrelated to the provision of plan benefits. In addition, it is an open question whether or not any or all accounts characterized as IRAs will meet the legal criteria for IRAs set out in federal statute. 26 U.S.C. §§ 408 and 408A.

[e] The law requires that there be a diverse array of private plan options available to employers, including life insurance plans designed for retirement purposes, Savings Incentive Match Plan for Employees (SIMPLE) IRA-type plans that provide for employer contributions, and payroll deduction IRAs to which employers do not contribute.

[f] Legislation explicitly includes self-employed individuals and sole proprietorships in the target employer group.

[g] Legislation provides for phased application of this requirement. Eligible employers are also required to allow open enrollment for employees who may voluntarily want to participate, and to periodically re-enroll employees who opt out.

[h] Legislation excludes employers that over the previous two years terminated an employer-sponsored retirement plan or ceased to offer an automatic deduction IRA.

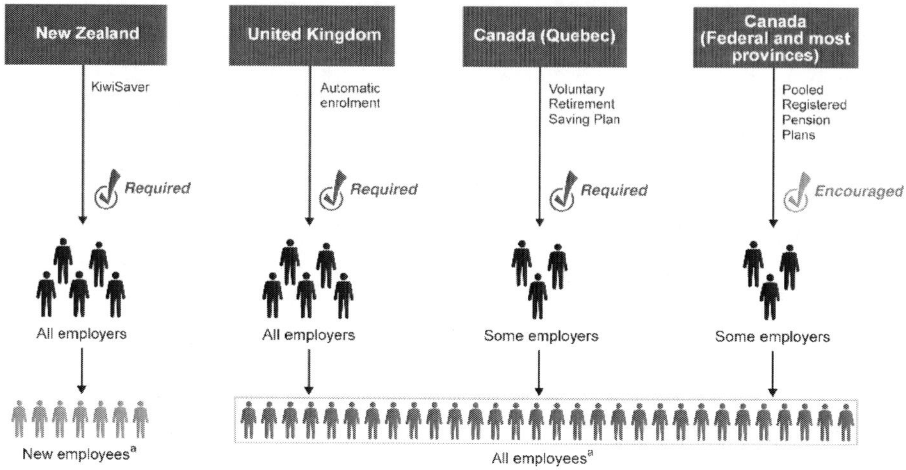

Source: GAO summary of documentation and testimonial evidence from knowledgeable international representatives. | GAO-15-556.

[a] Employee eligibility criteria and requirements are described in appendix V. Eligible employees are not required to participate and have the right to opt out.

Figure 8. Other Countries' Efforts to Expand Coverage in Workplace Retirement Savings Programs.

Automatic Enrollment

In combination with workplace access, each of the six state efforts we reviewed would require or allow employers to automatically enroll workers in a workplace retirement savings program to increase participation. Specifically, efforts in California, Illinois, and Maryland would require eligible employers that do not offer an employee benefit plan to automatically enroll their workers in the state-run program. In addition, state officials told us that the program for not-for-profit employers in Massachusetts would require employers who adopt the state plan to use automatic enrollment. In each of these programs, workers would have the ability to opt out. For example, California's Secure Choice program would require that employers enroll workers, but an official said workers would have a 90-day opt out period. In West Virginia, on the other hand, employers who would sign up to participate in the state-run program would have the option of automatically enrolling their workers, but it is at the employer's discretion. Similarly, Washington would provide an online marketplace with multiple vehicles—a SIMPLE IRA, payroll deduction IRA, and *my*RA—and employers that choose to use the marketplace would be encouraged, but not required, to automatically enroll workers.[75]

State officials and stakeholders emphasized the importance of automatic enrollment in increasing participation and contributions, which can, in turn, help reduce costs. For example, in California, members of the Secure Choice program's board said that automatic enrollment helps increase participation and promote better outcomes by nudging workers to save. A representative from the Maryland task force also said that without automatic enrollment fewer workers would participate, and the burden to provide financial education would increase. Similarly, our prior work and other research show that automatic enrollment is effective in overcoming workers' inertia and considerably increases participation.[76] For example, we previously found that automatic enrollment has considerably increased participation in programs adopting this feature, with some participation rates reaching as high as 95 percent.[77] In addition to expanding participation, state officials and stakeholders we interviewed said that automatic enrollment can reduce the costs of managing programs as the overall amount of savings increase.

Government officials and stakeholders in the countries we reviewed also emphasized the importance of automatic enrollment in increasing participation. According to the former Retirement Commissioner in New Zealand, automatic enrollment has been essential to the success of their KiwiSaver program and, without it, they would need a massive education campaign. Similarly, other government officials in New Zealand said that automatic enrollment is critical because too many people—even those who want to save—will not actively seek out participation. Government officials and stakeholders in the U.K. and Canada also highlighted the importance of automatic enrollment in increasing participation. According to a report to Parliament submitted by the largest organization representing unionized workers in the U.K., initial opt-out rates have been lower than expected, and their experience has shown the value of harnessing inertia to improve outcomes for workers. Moreover, the program was designed to further reduce opt-outs because it requires automatic re-enrollment of those who opted-out after 3 years.[78] Government officials in Canada said that the PRPP program utilizes automatic enrollment to increase participation, but it is unclear how successful it will be because the program is voluntary for employers.

Financial Incentives

While all six state efforts we reviewed anticipate using tax-advantaged vehicles to encourage participation, state officials and others said Roth IRAs, in particular, could help partially address concerns over limited tax benefits for lower-income workers. Financial incentives for participation in retirement savings programs include preferential tax treatment and employer contributions and multiple stakeholders noted that such incentives encourage worker participation. The state efforts we reviewed all seek to incentivize participation by using vehicles—employer sponsored 401(k) plans or workplace-based IRAs—that typically qualify for preferential tax treatment. But they do not allow for other financial incentives, such as employer contributions, or do so only to a limited extent.[79] In the absence of other financial incentives, some states, such as Illinois and California, are using or considering a Roth IRA vehicle to address concerns that lower-income workers may realize little or no current tax benefit from savings. Treasury officials and stakeholders said a Roth IRA may be beneficial for workers who have little or no current tax liability but may pay higher taxes in the future.[80] Moreover, Treasury officials said that Roth IRAs can benefit workers with limited resources by allowing them to withdraw contributions tax free under certain circumstances. In light of these issues, Illinois enacted the Secure Choice program, which uses a Roth IRA vehicle, and California's Secure Choice board commissioned a feasibility study to examine this issue.

Government officials and stakeholders in the countries we reviewed pointed to the importance of additional financial incentives, such as employer and government matching contributions, in increasing participation. For example, New Zealand's KiwiSaver used a one-time "kick-start" contribution of $1,000 New Zealand Dollars (NZD), about $650 U.S. dollars (USD), as well as matching employer contributions and tax benefits, as financial incentives to encourage worker participation in the program.[81] The former Retirement Commissioner in New Zealand and other stakeholders noted that the kick-start has been very popular and effective because it is so easily understood by participants, while the tax incentive is less well-understood. Government officials attributed the higher than expected rate of participation, particularly for those opting in to KiwiSaver, to the success of the financial incentives. Similarly, in the U.K., the automatic enrollment requirement includes matching contributions from the employer and government—employers are currently required to contribute 1 percent for a specified range of earnings, which will gradually increase to 3 percent in 2018, while the government contribution will increase from 0.2 percent to 1 percent. One academic noted that these matching contributions are very important for low-income workers who can only afford a modest contribution rate.

States Can Learn from Other Countries' Experiences Implementing another Key Strategy — Simplifying Administration and Investment Management

In addition to the key strategies discussed above, state efforts would take steps to simplify the overall design and implementation of their programs to reduce employer burden and complexity for workers. Specifically, in order to mitigate some of the challenges of setting up workplace retirement savings programs, state officials seek to (1) limit the responsibility and cost for employers, and (2) reduce complexity, cost, and investment risk for workers. These efforts would simplify program administration and investment management with the goals of lowering fees and encouraging broad employer adoption and worker participation. However, state officials also noted that this may elevate the role of the state in administering these programs and create implementation challenges, including how to fund them. Since no state effort has been implemented to date, states may be able to draw lessons from experiences in the countries we reviewed, as well as other state programs. (See appendix II for a full description of the actions states and other countries have taken to reduce administrative burden and cost for employers.)

To reduce administrative burden and cost for employers, states plan to take a number of actions that could offload or help employers with typical employer duties in workplace retirement savings programs (see fig. 9).

Other countries have taken similar steps to reduce administrative burdens and costs for employers. For example, the U.K. government created NEST to ensure that all employers, particularly small employers, would have access to a low-cost program, with the added benefit of diminishing the burden on employers of choosing an appropriate provider. NEST stakeholders said the existence of a low-cost program with a universal public service obligation[82] reduces the burden on small employers who might otherwise expend considerable time and effort in identifying a provider willing to serve them at an acceptable cost. Among other things, NEST's governing board selects and monitors providers, takes on fiduciary liability for management of the program's investments, and does not charge employers to set up and use NEST.[83] Lastly, NEST is responsible for sending out welcome packages to new participants with information on how to access the website and create accounts.[84]

Source: GAO analysis of state legislative records, documentation, and testimonial evidence from knowledgeable industry representatives. | GAO-15-556.

Note: See appendix II for a more detailed description of these steps for states and countries we reviewed—California, Illinois, Maryland, Massachusetts, Washington, West Virginia, Canada, New Zealand, and the United Kingdom.

[a] While all of the state efforts allow small employers of varying sizes to choose whether to participate in the state program, states define "small employer" differently. For example, states that are considering requiring employers to offer workplace access, such as California and Illinois, have exempted the smallest employers from the requirement—the law in Illinois exempts employers with fewer than 25 employees and the law in California exempts employers with fewer than 5 employees.

[b] Typical employer actions in this graphic are not meant to describe employer duties prescribed by the Employee Retirement Income Security Act of 1974 for fiduciaries of employee benefit plans.

Figure 9. Actions Selected States Intend to Take to Reduce Employers' Administrative Burden and Cost for Workplace Retirement Savings Programs.

In addition to addressing challenges for employers, state and country efforts we reviewed address issues of complexity, cost, and investment risk for workers through a variety of approaches (see table 3).

Table 3. Features in Selected State and Country Efforts to Reduce Complexity, Cost, and Investment Risk for Workers in Workplace Retirement Savings Programs

Strategy	Description	Potential Issues Cited by Stakeholders	Experience in Other Countries
Default contribution rate	Set default rate at an appropriate level to increase savings without causing too many workers to opt out (e.g., 3 percent for Illinois' Secure Choice).	•Default rate may not be sufficient to ensure adequate income. •To better ensure adequacy, California's Secure Choice program may include automatic escalation.	•In New Zealand, KiwiSaver's default contribution rate has changed several times and is currently set at 3 percent. Stakeholders said it was initially reduced from 4 percent to 2percent because some workers perceived the higher rate as unaffordable. However, most workers have remained at the default rate, which stakeholders said may not be sufficient. •The U.K. is phasing in an increase in the contribution rate for workers from 0.8 percent to 4 percent by 2018.
Structure investment options to limit choice and increase scale	Provide a diversified low-cost default fund and limit the number of investment options or pool funds into a single, professionally managed account.	•State efforts would limit worker choice to some degree. However, providing more choice would increase the program's burden to educate workers.	•In the U.K., the National Employment Savings Trust (NEST) uses a low-cost target date default fund and limits the number of additional investment options to five with varying levels of risk.

Table 3. (Continued)

Strategy	Description	Potential Issues Cited by Stakeholders	Experience in Other Countries
			One academic said that NEST's approach has dramatically driven down fees. In addition, a consumer advocate indicated that the limited number of investments also benefits participants by simplifying investment decisions.
Investment return guarantee	Provide some level of guaranteed return to minimize investment risk. The California Secure Choice board commissioned a feasibility study in January 2015 which will examine options for providing a guaranteed investment option.	•Cost of guarantee could reduce the overall rate of return. •Other strategies may provide more cost-effective ways to reduce risk, such as using a target date approach and shifting to low-risk assets as workers near retirement.	•The U.K.'s NEST default investment option is more conservatively invested during the initial period to avoid capital loss. This approach aims to normalize the habit of savings before introducing risk. •New Zealand's KiwiSaver default investment fund is conservatively invested to avoid capital loss. Government officials and stakeholders said, due to inertia, some workers may remain in the conservative fund even when it is more suitable for them to invest in options that provide the opportunity for higher risk and returns.

Strategy	Description	Potential Issues Cited by Stakeholders	Experience in Other Countries
Portability	Provide workers with a single account they can maintain when changing jobs (or working at multiple jobs) with participating employers.	•Full portability would be limited to within the state. •Increased portability may present a disadvantage for some employers who view their program as a retention tool.	•Programs we reviewed in Canada, New Zealand, and the U.K., to varying extents, allow workers to maintain the same account when they change jobs. •In New Zealand, workers are only allowed to have one KiwiSaver account which can be maintained when changing jobs. Government officials said that the centralized role of Inland Revenue, the country's tax office, in processing payroll deductions facilitates portability.
Limit on fees	Establish a limit on defined fees (e.g., 75 basis points for investment management fees in Illinois' Secure Choice program, 100 basis points in total annual fees in Washington's marketplace).	•Some providers may not participate if fee limit is too low. •Setting fee limit too high could reduce competitive pressure to lower fees.	•In addition to competitive pressure from NEST to lower fees, U.K. officials said the government decided to set a fee limit of 75 basis points for employer programs. However, one academic said that the fee limit may be hard to change once established and further noted that it is preferable to impose a broader responsibility on the governing board to ensure value for money.

Source: GAO analysis of state legislative records, documentation, and testimonial evidence from knowledgeable U.S. and international industry representatives. | GAO-15-556.

While Implementation of State Efforts Would Likely Increase Coverage, Some Private Sector Workers May Remain Uncovered

While successful implementation of these efforts by states will likely increase coverage for many private sector workers, some workers in those states may remain uncovered. In particular:

- **Workers at employers that continue to not offer access to a workplace retirement savings program**: While all the states that we reviewed would allow small employers of varying sizes and self-employed workers to choose whether to offer access to the state program to avoid creating a burden for these employers, many stakeholders felt this would leave some key worker populations uncovered. For state efforts that would create a voluntary program for all employers who are eligible to offer it to their workers, such as Massachusetts' not-for-profit program, stakeholders said many employers would still likely not choose to offer workplace access. Specifically, one national industry representative said, by definition, the employers targeted by state programs have already chosen not to offer retirement programs to their workers. Similarly, state and national stakeholders felt that the absence of a requirement for employers to offer workers access to workplace retirement savings programs would significantly lessen any expansion of coverage. Yet even those state efforts that would require eligible employers to offer workplace access, such as Illinois' and California's Secure Choice programs, would apply only to employers above a certain employee size threshold, 25 and 5 employees, respectively. According to one academic, there could be many employers under that size threshold. In addition, there are many self-employed workers who may continue not to have access to a workplace retirement program. For example, while California's target population is 6.3 million workers who lack access to an employer-sponsored plan, California Secure Choice board members estimated that there are an additional 2 million uncovered Californians who are contractors or self-employed. For this reason, California officials said that the Secure Choice program may allow self-employed workers to opt in.

- **Ineligible workers:** National industry stakeholders said that the state efforts would not cover some of the traditionally ineligible populations—including part-time and temporary workers—at employers that already offer qualifying employee benefit plans.[85] Some state efforts that would require employers of a certain size to offer workplace access, such as California and Illinois, exempt those employers that already offer employee benefit plans, for which existing law allows employers to determine which populations are eligible. By contrast, Maryland's proposed program would cover workers who are ineligible for the employee benefit plan offered by their employer, but only if the employer has 5 or more workers eligible for the state program.

  Workers who choose not to participate: Since none of the state efforts we studied would require workers to contribute—all of these efforts allow workers to either opt in or opt out—some workers will choose not to participate. As noted above, state efforts that would require the use of automatic enrollment will likely achieve broader increases in participation than efforts that allow workers to choose whether to opt in. For example, one industry study found that 41 percent of those surveyed postponed saving for retirement in order to pay down student loan debt.[86] In addition, a member of the California Secure Choice board said that some workers may not understand the value of earning investment returns on savings. To help address this, a California official said that the marketing materials for Secure Choice would need to clearly explain the benefits of participation.
- **Workers with very low earnings who cannot afford to participate**: Several stakeholders noted that it may be difficult for very low income workers to afford contributions. For example, a representative from the California Secure Choice board said that lower income workers may need the money for more immediate expenses. Our prior work indicates that while Social Security retirement benefits replace a higher percentage of earnings for lower income workers, this alone may not ensure an adequate retirement income.[87] In Canada, a representative of an association representing program providers said that the PRPP program is targeted to middle income workers, while lower income workers who are eligible for other federal government income supplements in retirement. Moreover, a representative of an employer group noted that the government is motivated to provide programs to ensure a minimum level of income in retirement because

Canadian provinces assume responsibility for the welfare of their citizens, and increased purchasing power can have a positive impact on the overall economy. In particular, outside of PRPP, Canada provides a targeted benefit, Guaranteed Income Supplement, which supplements the Canadian universal Old Age Security program to ensure low income seniors have a minimum level of income in retirement.

STATES FACE POTENTIAL CHALLENGES WITH LEGAL UNCERTAINTIES THAT COULD DELAY OR DETER THEIR EFFORTS TO EXPAND COVERAGE WITHOUT FEDERAL ACTION

States face legal uncertainty that could result in legal challenges in connection with efforts to expand coverage in workplace retirement savings programs for private sector workers, which will continue if no action is taken by Congress or relevant agencies, including DOL and Treasury.88 For over a decade legal uncertainty has influenced the design of state efforts. More recently, four of the six states we studied have enacted legislation to increase coverage in workplace retirement savings programs and legislators in other states have introduced similar bills or have studied potential solutions to expand coverage.[89] However, state and national stakeholders said these efforts face potential challenges because of legal uncertainties created by existing federal law—ERISA—and various agency regulations, depending on the type of program state efforts intend to create (see fig. 10).

ERISA Preemption

While stakeholders noted multiple issues causing legal uncertainties for state efforts, the most prevalent and pervasive was ERISA preemption. Specifically, ERISA preempts, or invalidates, any and all state laws that "relate to" any private-sector employee benefit plan.[90] Generally, the "relate to" provision in ERISA could be applicable to state laws that either directly regulate employee benefit plans or, in some cases, only indirectly affect such plans. For example, a state law that mandates the way in which employee benefit plans are administered may be determined to "relate to" such plans and may, therefore, be preempted. In this way, ERISA's preemption provision enables employers to establish uniform plans and administrative schemes, preventing them from having to comply with different requirements for employees located in different states. Whether ERISA preempts a state law has historically been determined by federal courts,[91] so states may face litigation. One national stakeholder indicated that it might be beneficial for a state to implement a program and go through resulting litigation to resolve some of the areas of legal uncertainty and clear the way for other states to implement similar programs. However, other state and national stakeholders were concerned about the potential consequences for workers and employers should an implemented program later be preempted. Noted implications for employers and workers included that the state program might lose its preferential tax treatment or create risk for employers that choose to offer the programs. Given these implications of uncertainty regarding ERISA preemption, state efforts to expand access to millions of workers and address the retirement savings shortfall may be delayed or deterred.

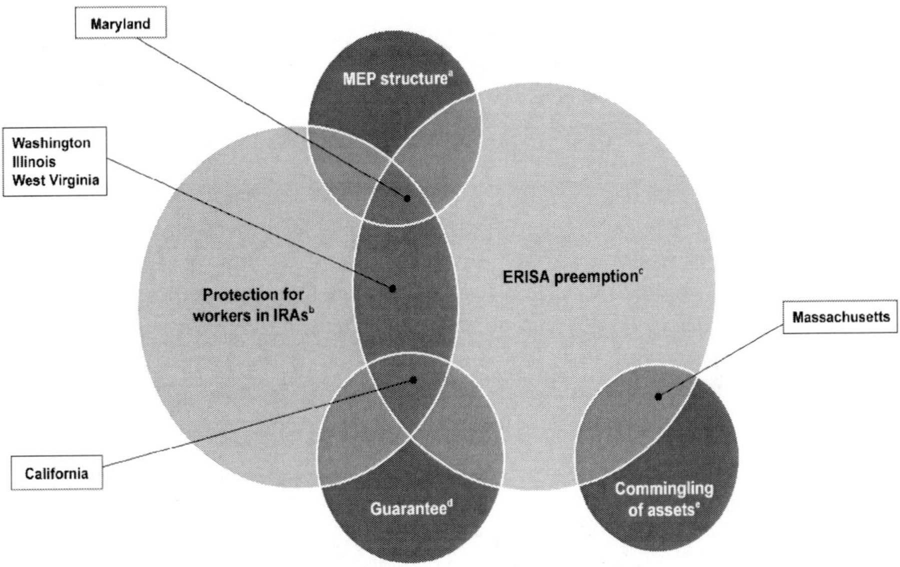

Source: GAO summary of interviews with state and national stakeholders and government officials. | GAO-15-556.

Note: This figure reflects the position of state efforts with respect to multiple areas of legal uncertainty identified through our review. Circle size indicates the number of states chosen for case studies that stakeholders noted were potentially affected by the issue causing uncertainty. For example, stakeholders from all 6 states reported that preemption under the Employee Retirement Income Security Act of 1974 (ERISA) is a concern, while for only one state (Maryland) was the current legal uncertainty regarding the structure of multiple employer plans (MEPs) mentioned as a concern (see table 4). To read this figure, follow the line from a state to see which legal uncertainties were identified in connection with each state effort. For example, Massachusetts was identified as a state that could face uncertainties related to ERISA preemption and comingling of assets. We selected these six states for case studies because they were identified as having "leading" state efforts by relevant government officials and knowledgeable industry representatives. For states that have enacted programs or marketplaces, we have focused on the issues potentially affecting those enacted programs in this figure. For the two states without enacted programs, Maryland and West Virginia, we identify the issues potentially affecting the state's most recent substantive legislative effort or other recent approaches stakeholders discussed. In addition to the 6 states we chose for case studies that are categorized in the graphic, some of the other 23 states we identified—listed in appendix IV—may experience these same issues causing similar uncertainties, depending on the type of programs these state efforts intend to create.

[a] Some states have considered using a MEP structure, but state and national stakeholders thought a state's ability to use this structure was uncertain because of conflicting Department of Labor (DOL) and Department of the Treasury (Treasury) regulations and concerns with MEP administration.

[b] If certain state efforts based on payroll deduction Individual Retirement Accounts (IRAs) are not determined to be employee benefit plans, according to some state and national stakeholders and government officials, there will be concerns about the inapplicability of certain worker protections and DOL oversight.

[c] Generally, ERISA preempts any state law relating to any employee benefit plan for private sector workers (29 U.S.C. § 1144(a)), which some stakeholders and DOL officials note causes significant uncertainty for these state programs.

[d] Stakeholders questioned the legal feasibility of providing participants with guaranteed returns for payroll deduction IRAs.

[e] It is uncertain whether states can pool assets of plans for private sector workers with those of public sector workers in a group trust without running afoul of relevant Treasury regulations regarding commingling of assets, or raising concerns under ERISA's fiduciary provisions.

Figure 10. Selected State Efforts to Increase Workplace Retirement Savings Program Coverage Face Multiple Issues that Could Cause Legal Uncertainty.

Based on our interviews with state and national stakeholders and government officials, none of the state efforts we reviewed are immune from legal uncertainty caused by ERISA preemption, but the type of uncertainty differs depending on the details of the state efforts.

- **Employee benefit plan programs**. For states that are attempting to use an employee benefit plan, such as a 401(k) plan or SIMPLE IRA, DOL officials told us that it is unclear whether a state could create a program without being preempted by ERISA because it is unclear what level of state effort would "relate to" employee benefit plans.[92] For example, Massachusetts is the furthest along implementing an effort that would create a 401(k) plan that not-for-profit employers with 20 or fewer employees could adopt, but national stakeholders had mixed opinions about whether its program will be preempted if legally challenged. Among other things, a Massachusetts official said that the state plans to take on administrative responsibilities and oversight of the program's service providers and will charge employers who choose to offer the program, but employers will still be plan fiduciaries.[93]
- **Payroll deduction IRA programs**. Partly to avoid uncertainty caused by ERISA preemption, four of the six states we examined would create programs using payroll deduction IRAs because by complying with relevant DOL regulations such IRAs are not employee benefit plans and are not subject to ERISA.[94] However, programs relying on payroll deduction IRAs could run into similar preemption uncertainty as state efforts with employee benefit plans because the DOL regulation does not address some key questions. First, the regulation was promulgated primarily to provide guidance to employers and, as DOL officials noted, it does not specify whether a state can offer payroll deduction IRAs to private sector workers. In addition, DOL officials said the regulation does not address whether certain program features states intend to use would cause the programs to be considered employee benefit plans.[95] For example, some states would like to capitalize on the potential advantages of using automatic enrollment for workers and requiring certain employers to offer workplace access to retirement savings programs. If these features cause the programs to be considered employee benefit plans, stakeholders said there would be uncertainty regarding preemption.

To address this uncertainty, state and national stakeholders thought DOL and Treasury should provide guidance and one thought DOL should clarify its regulation on payroll deduction IRAs.[96] On July 13, 2015, the President announced that DOL will propose a set of rules by the end of the year to provide a clear path forward for states to create retirement savings programs. DOL officials said the agency's role is limited under ERISA without further Congressional action—it can revise and promulgate regulations but there is nothing in ERISA that would allow it to waive preemption for state efforts. In one case, Illinois law explicitly requires the state to request an opinion or ruling from DOL on the status of the program with respect to ERISA before the program can be implemented. An Illinois stakeholder said that the state does not have to wait for a DOL opinion to implement the program, but implementation would stop if DOL sent a letter saying the Illinois program had to comply with ERISA.[97] While Illinois and other states may reach out to DOL for an opinion, in June 2015, DOL officials told us they had not received any such requests. Even if they did, DOL officials said the department does not have a formal process for issuing such opinions, and the opinion would not necessarily be binding in court. As a result, DOL's opinion may not give states the level of certainty regarding preemption they need to proceed.

Similarly, state and national stakeholders said state experimentation with various approaches could help determine which work best for expanding coverage in workplace retirement savings programs, so some have called for increased flexibility with respect to ERISA preemption. Given the need of many workers to increase their retirement savings, and limitations on DOL's ability to provide flexibility regarding ERISA preemption, stakeholders have suggested a number of ways to address uncertainty and facilitate state efforts to expand coverage in workplace retirement savings programs:

- **Amend ERISA's preemption provision**. Some stakeholders suggested Congress could amend ERISA's preemption provision by adding an exception for state efforts that expand coverage in workplace retirement savings programs.
- **Pilot program.** DOL officials told us a pilot program proposed in the Fiscal Year 2016 President's Budget Submission, issued February 2, 2015, could help identify actions states could take to effectively expand coverage in workplace retirement savings programs and determine if new, or changes to, DOL regulations or guidance are needed.[98] Under this proposal DOL would select a small number of states to implement different approaches to increasing coverage in workplace retirement savings programs. As part of such a pilot program, DOL officials said the department would need statutory authority from Congress to temporarily waive ERISA preemption for the pilot program timeframe in the selected states. They said some of

the appropriations DOL may receive pursuant to the program, should it be authorized, could be used to fund start-up costs for state efforts given the potential implementation challenges noted by states. A key part of the pilot program would also involve data collection on state efforts to provide government and experts an opportunity to see which strategies will actually increase coverage before making more permanent changes to permit state efforts.[99]

- **Safe harbor**. DOL and a national stakeholder said Congress could authorize DOL to establish a regulatory safe harbor for certain state efforts. DOL officials said the pilot program could even be considered a less permanent version of a safe harbor—albeit limited to a small number of states. To address other areas of legal uncertainty under ERISA, Congress has sometimes authorized DOL to prescribe safe harbors setting out conditions under which entities can operate without running afoul of the law. For example, PPA provided for DOL to prescribe by regulation a safe harbor for plans adopting automatic enrollment that, among other things, invest plan contributions in a qualified default investment alternative (QDIA).[100] DOL promulgated a regulation describing the type of investments that qualify as QDIAs.[101]

Other Issues Causing Legal Uncertainty

In addition to the uncertainty caused by ERISA preemption, state and national stakeholders and government officials shared other issues causing legal uncertainty. For example, DOL officials were concerned with states offering payroll deduction IRA programs because they would presumably fall outside of ERISA and DOL regulation. They said the protections provided by ERISA are important for employee benefit plan participants and that DOL has already developed a proven regulatory framework. Stakeholders said other legal uncertainty is caused by conflicting DOL and Treasury policies related to multiple employer plans, and questions about whether certain Treasury regulations allow states to implement a guaranteed return, or pool assets to achieve scale. For these other issues, states will continue to face uncertainty under existing DOL and Treasury regulations (see table 4).

Table 4. Other Issues Cited by Stakeholders that Cause Legal Uncertainty for State Efforts to Increase Workplace Retirement Savings Programs

Protection for workers in Individual Retirement Accounts (IRAs)	For state efforts that would create programs with payroll deduction IRAs, state and national stakeholders and government officials expressed concern about the inapplicability of the regulatory, oversight, and enforcement framework that the Department of Labor (DOL) has already developed for employee benefit plans—regarding disclosures, handling of employee contributions, and service provider arrangements, among other things.[a] Given these concerns, stakeholders said states may have to develop their own regulatory structure to protect participants in the state program.
Multiple Employer Plan (MEP) Structure	State and national stakeholders thought a state's ability to use a MEP was uncertain because DOL and Department of the Treasury (Treasury) regulations conflict regarding the ability of multiple unrelated employers to use a MEP structure. GAO has previously reported that while the Internal Revenue Service (IRS) has granted preferential tax treatment to some MEPs, DOL has taken the view that under ERISA only employers may establish or maintain a plan, and employers who sponsor a MEP must share control of the plan and an employment based common nexus or other organizational relationship unrelated to the provision of benefits.[b] In addition, stakeholders cited certain concerns with MEP administration, which need to be addressed to protect workers against losses and fraud before states can be certain about the legal feasibility of using this structure.
Guarantee	Some stakeholders questioned whether providing participants with guaranteed returns, a feature proposed in California's law, would prevent the program from qualifying as an IRA. Guarantee and other annuity-like features may make these accounts look like defined benefit plans in which the state program, not the individual workers, bears the investment risk. California's legal feasibility study will answer these questions before the program can be implemented.[c]
Commingling assets with other state programs	Some states may attempt to achieve scale by capitalizing on the size of retirement plans for public workers and pooling funds for both programs, but stakeholders said it remains to be seen whether this approach will be approved pursuant to relevant Treasury guidance regarding the commingling of funds from public and private sector programs.[d] A Massachusetts official told us Massachusetts plans to utilize this approach, but as of June 2015 was still waiting for final Treasury approval.

Source: GAO summary of interviews with state and national stakeholders and government officials. | GAO-15-556.

[a] DOL administers and enforces Title I of the Employee Retirement Income Security Act of 1974 (ERISA). DOL has issued guidance to employers related to payroll deduction IRAs regarding when such an arrangement would not be an employee benefit plan subject to DOL's jurisdiction. As long as employers follow guidelines set by DOL for managing payroll deduction IRAs, employers are not subject to the fiduciary requirements in ERISA Title I that apply to employee benefit plans, such as 401(k) plans. Similarly, for state efforts that would use Savings Incentive Match Plan for Employees (SIMPLE) IRAs, DOL noted that because these are IRAs, they are not subject to the full range of ERISA protections.

[b] DOL Advisory Opinion 2012-04A, May 25, 2012. GAO. *Private Sector Pensions: Federal Agencies Should Collect Data and Coordinate Oversight of Multiple Employer Plans*. (Washington, D.C., Sept. 13, 2012). GAO-12-665.

[c] California's Secure Choice board decided to put in place a two-step procurement process to separate the legal analysis and market feasibility study required by enacted legislation. In addition, the California law prohibits implementation of the program if the IRA arrangements offered fail to qualify for favorable tax treatment ordinarily accorded to IRAs.

[d] IRS Rev. Rul. 2011-1, 2011-1 C.B. 251.

CONCLUSION

Millions of workers in the United States have little or no retirement savings, an issue exacerbated by the lack of access to workplace retirement savings programs for many of them. Without this coverage, a significant number of Americans face the prospect of financial insecurity in retirement, and federal and state safety net programs face the potential for bearing increased financial burdens. Despite several major changes to federal law during the last few decades, federal action has not spurred such an increase in coverage. Recognizing this need to increase coverage, and thereby increase retirement savings, some states have undertaken efforts that would require or encourage employers to expand access to workplace retirement savings programs. However, the existing framework of federal law and regulation was not designed to foster a state role in providing coverage to private sector workers, and the resulting uncertainties about the application of that framework raise questions about the future and success of such efforts. Changes at the federal level—Congressional action combined with revised regulations and guidance within the authority of relevant agencies, particularly DOL— could help address these uncertainties. These actions would require difficult policy choices and involve weighing the benefits of uniformity and consistency provided by ERISA preemption against the potential value of state efforts to adopt innovative approaches to address the lack of sufficient retirement savings by their citizens. Moreover, along with the known regulatory challenges already identified by state officials and experts we interviewed, other areas of uncertainty could emerge through the experience of states implementing these programs.

Congress has several options for legislative action, each of which highlight some of the difficult policy choices and trade-offs that would need to be considered. For example, amending the ERISA preemption provision to add exceptions for any of the state efforts discussed here would provide states with certainty about which types of efforts they could undertake. It might also set a precedent for additional exceptions that could diminish the nationwide uniformity and stability the preemption provision is intended to create. Alternatively, a pilot program could permit states to test, with DOL involvement, innovative approaches to increasing coverage. However, by their very nature, pilot programs involve a limited number of states and therefore would not create certainty for states not included in the pilot that wish to expand coverage. Pilot programs are generally temporary in nature so even included states may not have the benefit of long-term certainty about the feasibility of their efforts. Finally, through the creation of a statutorily authorized safe harbor, DOL could identify a small number of options available to states that would not run afoul of ERISA's preemption provision, thereby retaining some degree of ERISA uniformity for employers. However, the development of a safe harbor option that would appeal to states and employers while retaining key protections for workers could be challenging, and little is known about the relative effectiveness of any particular model to actually increase coverage and retirement savings.

MATTER FOR CONGRESSIONAL CONSIDERATION

To address the legal uncertainty stemming from ERISA preemption of state laws while maintaining the advantages of ERISA for both employers and workers, Congress should consider providing states limited flexibility to pursue efforts to increase coverage under workplace retirement savings programs. To do this, Congress could, for example, direct or authorize the Secretary of Labor, in consultation with the Secretary of the Treasury, to (1) promulgate regulations prescribing a limited safe harbor under which state workplace retirement savings programs with sufficient safeguards would not be preempted and would receive tax treatment comparable to that provided to private sector workplace retirement savings programs, or (2) create a pilot program under which DOL could select a limited number of states to establish workplace retirement savings programs subject to DOL and Treasury oversight. In either case, any such initiative should ensure that state programs include adequate participant protections and are subject to agency oversight, appropriate reporting requirements, and meaningful evaluation.

RECOMMENDATION FOR EXECUTIVE ACTION

To facilitate state efforts to expand coverage in workplace retirement savings programs, we recommend that the Secretary of Labor and Secretary of the Treasury consider their authority and review and revise, if necessary, existing regulations and guidance causing uncertainty for state efforts. For example, the Secretary of Labor could direct the Employee Benefits Security Administration's (EBSA) Assistant Secretary to revise Interpretive Bulletin 99-1 to clarify whether states can offer payroll deduction Individual Retirement Accounts (IRAs) and, if so, whether features in relevant enacted state legislation—such as automatic enrollment and/or a requirement that employers offer a payroll deduction—would cause these programs to be treated as employee benefit plans.

AGENCY COMMENTS AND OUR EVALUATION

We provided a draft of this report to DOL, Treasury, the Pension Benefit Guarantee Corporation (PBGC), and the Social Security Administration (SSA) for their review and comment. PBGC and SSA did not provide comments. DOL provided written comments, DOL also provided technical comments, which we have incorporated where appropriate. Treasury provided oral and written technical comments, which we have incorporated where appropriate. Treasury generally agreed with the findings, conclusions, and recommendation of this report.

In its written comments, DOL generally agreed with the findings and conclusions of the report. They noted that inadequate retirement savings has a detrimental impact on the well-being of older Americans and increases the burden on state and federal retirement income support programs. In addition,

DOL noted that many of the states engaged in efforts to address this issue by expanding coverage in workplace retirement savings programs have questions about preemption by ERISA.

DOL generally agreed with the recommendation of the report. To address uncertainty facing state efforts, EBSA is initiating a regulatory agenda entitled "Saving Arrangements Established by States for Non-Governmental Employees," which will appear in the Fall 2015 Semi-Annual Regulatory Agenda. EBSA expects to publish a Notice of Proposed Rulemaking by the end of 2015. We agree that DOL should review and revise existing regulations and guidance to accomplish all that can be done administratively to facilitate state efforts to expand coverage

Sincerely yours,

Charles A. Jeszeck
Director, Education, Workforce,
and Income Security

APPENDIX I: OBJECTIVES, SCOPE, AND METHODOLOGY

Our objectives for this study were to examine: (1) recent estimates of workplace retirement savings program coverage, including eligibility and participation, and characteristics of workers who lack coverage, (2) strategies used by states and other countries to expand coverage among private sector workers, and (3) potential challenges states could face given existing federal law and regulations.

To answer our research objectives, we used several different approaches. We examined data on private sector workers. We reviewed relevant research, selected state and federal legislation,[1] and federal laws, regulations, and guidance. In addition, we interviewed state, national, and international industry stakeholders and government officials, including those at the Department of Labor's (DOL) Employee Benefits Security Administration, the Department of the Treasury (Treasury), the Pension Benefit Guaranty Corporation, and the Social Security Administration (SSA). Section 1 describes the information sources and empirical methods we used to examine workplace access and participation across various characteristics of workers. Section 2 describes the methodology by which we identified state efforts and selected case studies, and reviewed the strategies they use and the potential challenges they could face. Section 3 describes similar methodology for our international review.

Section 1: Examining Estimates of Retirement Program Access and Participation and Characteristics of Workers Who Lack Coverage

To answer this question, we obtained information from the Survey of Income and Program Participation (SIPP) along with taxpayer data from W-2 filings, reviewed relevant literature, and conducted interviews with academics, industry stakeholders, and agency officials.

SIPP and IRS/SSA data

SIPP is a nationally representative survey conducted by the U.S. Census Bureau. This panel survey is conducted generally every 4 years and resurveys participants every 4 months in a series of "waves" for the duration of their panel. Within each wave, Census administers a core survey consisting of questions that are asked at every interview, and several modules relating to a particular topic. We used data from the core survey and the topical module on retirement and pension coverage fielded from January-April 2012, the most recent data available. The survey collected data on about 52,000 individuals, including detailed information on work history, demographics, assets, and income.

In comparison to other nationally representative surveys, SIPP has several main advantages. First, SIPP collects separate information on defined benefit (DB) and defined contribution (DC) plans. Other surveys, such as the Current Population Survey, do not distinguish between income from and participation in DB and DC plans. Second, the SIPP sample is larger than comparable surveys, such as the Survey of Consumer Finances (SCF). Consequently, it is possible to produce point estimates for demographic subcategories with a higher degree of reliability. Further, in comparison to SCF, which oversamples wealthy households, SIPP oversamples lower-income households—arguably an important component of an analysis of income security.

Despite its advantages, SIPP has two limitations for our analysis. First, as with most survey data, SIPP data are self-reported. This can be problematic for the reporting of data on income sources and retirement program participation. For example, respondents might incorrectly report that they participate in a workplace retirement savings program when they do not. Second, despite the fact that SIPP differentiates between participation in a DB or DC plan, it does not contain full information on whether an individual's employer offers a DB plan.[2]

Previous research has also found evidence of under-reporting of retirement program participation by comparing self-reported survey responses to W-2 tax records.[3] Specifically, W-2 records include information on contributions to tax-advantaged retirement programs. By comparing the SIPP data to W-2 tax records, researchers can identify under-reporting of program participation. Similar to the approach used in prior research, we worked with Census to create a W-2 adjusted indicator of participation. If a respondent reported they did not participate, but actually had positive contributions to a workplace retirement program reported on their W-2, they were re-classified as participating. The data did not allow us to correct for the possibility that some participants may report they are participating when in fact they did not. Specifically, if the respondent said "yes, they do participate" but there is no contribution evident in the W-2, we did not recode them as a no because we cannot rule out the possibility that their employer offers a defined benefit plan or defined contribution plan in which only the employer contributes.

Data Reliability

We conducted a data reliability assessment of selected SIPP variables by conducting electronic data tests for completeness and accuracy, reviewing documentation on the dataset, or interviewing knowledgeable officials about how the data are collected and their appropriate uses. For the purposes of our analysis, we found the variables we ultimately reported on to be sufficiently reliable.

We compared our estimates to estimates provided by Census using the SIPP data linked to tax records on retirement program contributions. Census replicated our analysis using the public use SIPP data with consistent results. Further, the results of our regression analysis of participation using the self-reported measure in the public use data and the W-2 adjusted measure were very similar in the size and significance of variables included in our analysis.

Methods for Examining Retirement Program Coverage

In our sample we included respondents who are age 18 and older working in private sector jobs. For all SIPP analyses, we used SIPP individual-level weights to compute point estimates. Table 5 provides an overview of the number of private sector workers participating in workplace retirement savings programs using the W-2 adjusted data.

Table 5. Estimated Number of Private Sector Workers Participating or Not in a Workplace Retirement Savings Program by Characteristic, 2012

		Participating	Not participating	Total
Income	Lowest quartile	5,625,260	19,944,105	**25,569,365**
	2nd quartile	11,293,685	14,199,960	**25,493,645**
	3rd quartile	17,053,194	8,590,707	**25,643,901**
	Highest quartile	21,381,170	4,194,392	**25,575,562**
Firm size	More than 1,000 employees	30,280,100	14,053,868	**44,333,968**
	501 to 1,000 employees	3,110,245	1,711,840	**4,822,085**
	101 to 500 employees	8,087,690	4,999,187	**13,086,877**
	51 to 100 employees	3,590,040	3,435,478	**7,025,518**
	50 or fewer employees	10,267,361	22,746,663	**33,014,024**
Work hours	Part time	10,684,855	20,833,892	**31,518,747**
	Full time	44,651,910	26,111,815	**70,763,725**
Occupation	Management, business, science, and arts	23,766,398	9,151,051	**32,917,449**
	Service	5,299,478	13,165,601	**18,465,079**
	Sales and office	14,701,802	12,473,433	**27,175,235**
	Natural resources, construction, and maintenance	4,270,927	5,348,277	**9,619,204**
	Production, transportation, and material moving	7,320,757	6,784,747	**14,105,504**
Age	18-24	2,816,783	10,407,552	**13,224,335**
	25-54	41,120,368	29,170,859	**70,291,227**
	55-64	9,693,698	5,219,684	**14,913,382**
	65 and older	1,722,527	2,131,002	**3,853,529**

Source: GAO analysis of 2012 data from the Survey of Income and Program Participation (SIPP) and the U.S. Census Bureau. | GAO-15-556.

To determine the extent to which private sector workers are covered by workplace retirement savings programs and the characteristics of those who lack coverage, we reviewed relevant literature and interviewed researchers, stakeholders, and agency officials to discuss relevant research methodologies and findings. This review informed our analysis of SIPP and Census data. Specifically, we examined the likelihoods, or odds, of the following outcomes: 1) participating in a retirement program (among all private sector workers), 2) having an employer that offers a retirement program (among all private sector workers), 3) being eligible (among those offered programs), and 4) participating in a program (among those who are eligible). The regression models we used to estimate these likelihoods included variables for the following characteristics of workers: income, occupation, education, age, gender, marital status, race/ethnicity, size of the firm they worked for, whether they worked full-time or part-time, whether they worked for the full year or only part of the year, and whether they were or were not union members. We examined regression results from the SIPP public-use data and the linked W-2 data. As described in the body of this report and appendix VI, the results were very similar in the size and significance of variables included in our analysis for both measures of participation.

Literature Review and Interviews

To understand factors that may be associated with access to workplace retirement programs and inform the methodology for our study, we conducted a literature review. A formal literature search was conducted by a GAO reference librarian using the Proquest database. In addition, we coordinated with the Congressional Research Service and Congressional Budget Office to identify relevant studies, and checked with DOL and SSA officials as to whether they would recommend any additional materials. Finally, during interviews with outside researchers, we asked for recommendations for other noteworthy studies. We performed these searches and identified articles from June 2014 to September 2014.

Our review primarily focused on studies from the last five years (2009-2014). The team reviewed article abstracts and identified those which were most relevant to our research objectives and developed detailed spreadsheet summaries of study goals, methodology, and findings.

Section 2: Examining Strategies Used in State Efforts to Expand Coverage and the Potential Challenges States Could Face Given Existing Federal Law and Regulations

To review the strategies used in state efforts[4] to expand private sector retirement coverage and the potential challenges they could face given existing federal law and regulations, we compiled a list of recent state efforts and conducted case studies in six states.

List of State Efforts

To provide context on the number and type of recent state efforts we (1) developed a list of recent efforts in 29 states by reviewing industry websites and publications, interviewing federal officials and knowledgeable industry representatives, and conducting targeted searches of legislative databases; (2) confirmed the completeness of the list of states we identified at multiple points during the process with knowledgeable stakeholders; and (3) described the strategies in these state efforts. See appendix IV for a full description of our methodology and results.

State Case Studies

We selected a limited number of state efforts for case studies in October 2014 to provide non-generalizable examples of the types of efforts underway to expand coverage. To do so, we asked officials from DOL and Treasury and representatives from the Pension Rights Center, the American Society of Pension Professionals and Actuaries, and the retirement issues group AARP to recommend "leading" state efforts. They recommended eight states: California, Connecticut, Illinois, Maryland, Massachusetts, Oregon, Washington, and West Virginia. From those eight states, we selected six for case studies based on the following criteria:

- States that enacted, or were expected to enact, legislation that leads to implementation of a substantive effort to expand coverage.
- Some parity in the numbers of states from each of the two broad categories of state efforts we initially identified—automatic IRA- and other voluntary account-type programs.
- State efforts with some differences in how the broad categories were approached.

Based on these criteria, we selected California, Illinois, Maryland, Massachusetts, Washington, and West Virginia. We did not select Oregon because the state's Retirement Savings Task Force had just completed a study that recommended the program have certain characteristics,[5] but any legislative proposal that might utilize those recommendations would not be available until 2015 at the earliest. We did not select Connecticut because its recent legislation and historical context were similar to other states we selected.

To conduct case studies in the six states, we reviewed applicable GAO and academic research and legislative documentation on each state's effort. Where available, we reviewed status updates and final reports by the state government or appointed task force or board. In addition, we interviewed national industry stakeholders and academics with knowledge of state efforts, and key stakeholders in the states including, where applicable, elected state officials, state government officials, board or task force members, and employer, worker, and industry representatives. We asked about key features of the state efforts and advantages, disadvantages, and challenges of the strategies in the state efforts. We conducted some of these interviews in person in California, Illinois, and Washington.

Section 3: Examining Strategies Used in Other Countries' Efforts to Expand Coverage

To examine strategies used by other countries to expand coverage and identify lessons learned for the United States, we studied efforts in three countries that have voluntary workplace retirement systems—Canada, New Zealand, and the United Kingdom (U.K.).[6] Our review provides non-generalizable examples of the types of efforts underway to expand coverage outside the U.S. We conducted an initial review of workplace retirement savings programs in Organisation for Economic Co-operation and Development (OECD) countries and consulted with knowledgeable industry stakeholders at the OECD and World Bank, among others. Given this information, we selected countries that met the following criteria:

- Private sector, workplace retirement savings programs are an important pillar of the country's retirement system.
- The country has well-developed financial markets.
- Reforms designed to increase coverage have been implemented or are in the process of being implemented.
- Reforms use similar strategies as state efforts we identified. Specifically, the reforms use a voluntary approach or require employers to offer a program but allow workers to opt out.

- It was identified through our research and the consensus of knowledgeable external stakeholders as having strong potential for yielding useful lessons for the United States.
- It is not duplicative. Where similar programs exist in multiple countries we will select the one that best addresses the other selection criteria.

As part of our review, we examined available documentation and analyzed the selected countries' systems based on strategies used to increase coverage and the potential effectiveness in the United States. In particular, we examined eligibility and enrollment features, as well as measures targeted to workers who tend to lack coverage (e.g., those who work for small employers or are self-employed). We interviewed knowledgeable industry stakeholders and government officials from each country, as well as academics and national stakeholders based in the United States, about each strategy's strengths, weaknesses, tradeoffs, and lessons learned for the United States.

We did not conduct an independent legal analysis to verify the information provided about the laws, regulations, or policies of the countries selected for this study. Instead, we relied on appropriate secondary sources, interviews, and other sources to support our work. We submitted key report excerpts to agency officials in each country for their review and verification, and we incorporated their technical corrections as necessary. We note also that the fact that a legal feature was successful in one or more of the countries we visited, which may have significantly different cultures, histories, and legal systems than the United States, does not necessarily indicate that it would be successful in the United States.

We conducted this performance audit from June 2014 through September 2015 in accordance with generally accepted government auditing standards. Those standards require that we plan and perform the audit to obtain sufficient, appropriate evidence to provide a reasonable basis for our findings and conclusions based on our audit objectives. We believe that the evidence obtained provides a reasonable basis for our findings and conclusions based on our audit objectives.

APPENDIX II: DESCRIPTION OF EFFORTS TO SIMPLIFY ADMINISTRATION AND INVESTMENT MANAGEMENT OF WORKPLACE RETIREMENT SAVINGS PROGRAMS

Reducing Administrative Burden and Cost for Employers

Use Employers' Existing Payroll Processes

States we reviewed would attempt to use employers' existing payroll processes to reduce administrative burden for employers, but some stakeholders said this may create challenges that could be mitigated based on state experience with other programs. For example, Maryland's Task Force found that the best way to minimize administrative burden on small employers is to use their existing payroll process.[1] While some stakeholders were concerned with employers' payroll deduction capabilities, research shows that the majority of employers already use electronic payroll services.[2] Because of this, state and national stakeholders told us that deducting and remitting contributions from a worker's paycheck would not substantially increase the burden or cost for most employers. However, California stakeholders noted that using employers' existing payroll processes would create a large state role in educating employers about their responsibilities and collecting payroll deductions. For example, the California Secure Choice program would need to be able to accept contributions from millions of small employers and one stakeholder noted that the program would likely have to deal with privacy issues if employers use tax identification information to remit payments.[3] However, some states hoped to utilize the experience of state agencies that accept payroll deduction for other employer deductions and payments. For example, board members said that the California Secure Choice program may utilize the services of the state's Employment Development Department that already collects employment taxes from employers in the state. While implementation details still need to be decided, board members hoped to capitalize on the department's connection with California employers, infrastructure for processing payroll deductions, and experience with enforcing employer requirements. Similarly, Illinois' Department of Revenue currently oversees employers' payroll deposits for taxes, so Illinois stakeholders thought that the Illinois Secure Choice program might be able to leverage its administrative and enforcement experience.

Government officials and stakeholders in New Zealand noted that this approach has worked well for KiwiSaver. Inland Revenue, New Zealand's tax collection agency, is the interface between employers and providers, which officials said simplifies the administrative role for employers. Employers do not have to engage with various KiwiSaver providers a worker may select nor administer worker requests for opting out. Employers simply send a worker's contributions to Inland Revenue and the agency sends the worker's contribution to their KiwiSaver provider.

Allow Small Employers to Choose Whether to Participate and Other Efforts to Recognize Resource Limitations of Small Employers

In recognition of resource limitations for small employers, all of the state efforts would allow small employers of varying sizes to choose whether to participate in the state program. While stakeholders and research indicate that payroll deduction is readily accessible for the majority of employers, some of the smallest employers may not yet have migrated to an electronic payment system. As a result, each of these state efforts allows the smallest employers to choose whether to participate in the program. In particular, states that are considering requiring employers to offer workplace access have exempted the smallest employers from the requirement, but would allow them to choose to offer access to the program. For example, Illinois law exempts employers with fewer than 25 employees and California law exempts employers with fewer than 5 employees.[4] Stakeholders did note a drawback to allowing small employers—as well as self-employed workers—to choose whether to offer the state program. Specifically, if too few employers choose to offer a purely voluntary program, it may not be able to achieve the scale necessary to ensure that costs are reasonable.[5]

In contrast, some of the countries we studied required even small employers to offer workplace access but they took other actions to recognize the resource limitations of small employers, including phasing in the employer requirement and creating specific programs that support small employers. For example, in the U.K. the employer requirement to offer access and automatically enroll workers is being phased in gradually between October 2012 and February 2018 based on employer size, which provides smaller employers additional time to prepare for meeting the new requirements.[6] However, without any other action by the government, U.K officials concluded that small employers may find it difficult to meet the automatic enrollment requirements because of a supply gap—the Pensions Commission concluded that existing providers would find it unprofitable to serve employers that did not previously offer workers access, the overwhelming majority of which had fewer than 15 employees, at a reasonable cost to workers.[7] To address the supply gap, it created the National Employment Savings Trust (NEST) to ensure that all employers, particularly small employers, would have access to a low-cost program, with the added benefit of diminishing the burden on employers of choosing an appropriate provider (see text box 1). Similarly, the Australian government recognized the specific needs of small employers by creating a Small Business Superannuation Clearing House in 2010 to simplify administrative requirements and lessen the administrative burden on small employers. The Clearing House is a free service that allows eligible employers to make one payment at least quarterly on behalf of all of the employer's workers. The Clearing House then disburses the payments to each of the worker's choice of fund (see text box 2).

Text Box 1

The United Kingdom's National Employment Savings Trust (NEST) has a public service obligation to accept any employer (and any qualifying worker) that wishes to use it, and in this way serves all those employers and workers who are unable to find another provider of a retirement savings program. The existence of a low-cost program with a universal public service obligation reduces the burden on small employers who might otherwise expend considerable time and effort in identifying a provider willing to serve them at an acceptable cost. In addition, there are no charges for employers to set up and use NEST. Finally, NEST has worked with the major payroll software providers in the United Kingdom to integrate their platforms with NEST in order to reduce data compliance burdens on employers. NEST representatives thought that this effort could make NEST even easier to use for small employers.

Source: GAO summary of interviews with NEST representatives and the Department for Work and Pensions review, *Making Automatic Enrolment Work*, October 2010.

Text Box 2

Australian officials explained that the Small Business Superannuation Clearing House was set up to help employers make contributions on behalf of their workers as required by the Australian Superannuation system. They thought that these contributions could represent a heavy administrative burden for small employers because workers are allowed to choose the provider to which they want the employer to send their contributions, employers must make payments at least quarterly, and superannuation providers all have slightly different forms and payment delivery methods. Created in 2010, the purpose of the Small Business Superannuation Clearing House was to simplify administrative requirements, lessening the administrative burden for small employers— those with 19 or fewer workers or, from July 1, 2015, those with total income of less than $2 million Australian dollars (AUD) (about $1.4 million USD). Employers log onto the Clearing House's website and are required to complete a one-time registration, after which their involvement is low. As of July 31, 2015, about 120,000 employers are registered to use the service, approximately 15 percent of those eligible. The majority of employers who use the service generally have between 3 and 19 workers. The government has found that these employers typically do not have payroll software. Officials said that employers who use the Clearing House say it saves them time and gives them peace of mind because use of the system guarantees they have met their obligation. The Clearing House is funded through government appropriations and costs the government about $6 million AUD annually.

Source: GAO summary of interviews with Australian Stakeholders.

Other Actions to Reduce Administrative Burden for Employer

States would also take other actions to reduce administrative burden for employers and may be able to learn from other countries' implementation experiences, especially those of NEST in the U.K., and their own experiences with other state savings programs, including college savings plans and public pension plans (see table 6).

Table 6. Other Actions State Efforts Would Take to Reduce Administrative Burden for Employers Offering Access to Workplace Retirement Savings Programs

State Actions	Description	Experience in Other Countries and Other State Programs
Selecting and monitoring providers	•Most state programs, including Illinois, California, and Massachusetts, would specify that the program's governing body will select and monitor providers for the program.	In the United Kingdom (U.K.), its NEST program's governing board selects and monitors providers.

Table 6. (Continued)

State Actions	Description	Experience in Other Countries and Other State Programs
	•Washington's program would require a state agency to approve providers, reducing some employer responsibilities in selecting and monitoring providers, although employers would still need to select from those providers—they would be required to access the marketplace website and pick the option they want to offer workers.	In Canada and New Zealand, service providers are licensed by the government to offer qualifying plans. For example, financial institutions that want to provide Pooled Registered Pension Plans (PRPPs) for employers in federally regulated industries in Canada are required to be licensed by the federal Office of the Superintendent of Financial Institutions.
Provide educational materials and disclosures for workers	States plan to reduce administrative burden for employers related to worker outreach by providing information and educational materials. For example, state stakeholders thought the following information should be provided to workers: •What they are investing in and how fees are charged •Explanation that they can access savings in event of a hardship •Explanation that their employer's role is limited—employers are not liable for investment returns •How the program compares to products on the retail market California and Illinois stakeholders noted that these materials would have to be customized to overcome language and cultural barriers.	In the U.K., NEST is responsible for sending out "welcome" packages to new participants with information on how to access the website and create accounts. NEST also has online tools including communication templates and electronic member options for opt-outs to make it easier for employers. In 2012, NEST also issued a pension "jargon buster" to help make pensions understandable to individuals. In addition, experience from other state programs might help states prepare educational materials and disclosures for workers. For example, California stakeholders noted that its college savings plan program and health care exchange had gained valuable experience in marketing and outreach to increase worker participation. Similarly, a stakeholder in Massachusetts noted that the Treasurer's office has experience meeting ERISA's participant disclosure requirements because it has tried to comply with

State Actions	Description	Experience in Other Countries and Other State Programs
		ERISA for its deferred compensation plan for public workers even though it was not required.
Limit employer liability	State efforts may take actions to limit employer liability related to the state programs. For example, some states would: •Include specific language in legislation acknowledging that employers would not be liable for investments in the program nor for making investment-related decisions. •Use payroll deduction IRAs, instead of employee benefit plans, which stakeholders believe exposes employers to less potential liability than employee benefit plans.	In the U.K., NEST is a not-for-profit entity that is the trustee for the program and takes on fiduciary liability for management of the program's investments. KiwiSaver providers in New Zealand and PRPP providers in Canada all take on trustee or fiduciary liability. In addition government agencies in these countries provide some level of oversight over providers.
Reduce or eliminate employer administrative costs, including employer contributions	Stakeholders noted that reducing administrative costs for employers could encourage employers to voluntarily offer the program. Washington plans to completely eliminate employer administrative costs by requiring all costs be paid through participant fees, limited to 1 percent. In addition, some state efforts use payroll deduction IRAs, which do not allow for employer contributions. Other states that would use employee benefit plans allow voluntary employer contributions.	In New Zealand, the government subsidizes small employer administrative costs. The tax agency administers the program but does not charge employers that use its services. The U.K. decided to require that employers contribute, but phased in contribution levels to reduce the burden. Specifically, minimum employer contributions are being implemented in three phases from 2012 to 2018. Starting in October 2012, employers contributed 1 percent of qualifying earnings. Employer contribution levels will increase in October 2017 and finally in October 2018, when employers will need to remit required minimum contributions of 3 percent.

Source: GAO summary of information from interviews with state and country stakeholders and relevant research. | GAO-15-556.

These actions to reduce administrative burden for employers elevate the state's role in the programs, which could create implementation challenges, including how to fund state actions. Stakeholders generally noted the importance of the state's acceptance of some of the employer's administrative duties and liability in encouraging employers to offer workplace access.[8] However, this state role is particularly important for efforts that would require eligible employers to participate, such as in California, Illinois, and Maryland. While enabling legislation provides the intent and the direction of these state programs, the state effort's governing body will have to make many decisions to develop and implement the programs, including how to educate employers about their responsibilities.[9] In three of the four states we studied that had enacted such legislation—Massachusetts, California, and Illinois—the states have already taken or planned at least 2 years to study options and design their programs.[10] In addition, stakeholders noted that the six states we reviewed would likely incur potentially significant startup and ongoing costs and saw potential challenges in determining how to fund those costs.[11] For example, a California official expects the feasibility study and related legal analysis will cost $1 million, but total startup costs could be much larger. Since the feasibility study has to be funded without a state appropriation, the state official said that an immediate challenge was to raise the necessary funds for the feasibility study so they could better determine cost estimates for developing the program and ongoing administration. The U.K. recently dealt with this issue when it created NEST and received a loan from the government. A NEST representative said it had spent about 300 million British pounds (GBP) (about $459 million USD) over the last 2.5 years to (1) develop systems infrastructure and architecture; (2) enroll employers; and (3) fund the program in the first few years while contributions are very low. For the latter, the NEST representative said that current members are contributing 2 percent of their generally low wage—at these rates contributions could be 20 GBP (about $31 USD) a month—so NEST does not receive revenue from these accounts to pay back the loan and, in fact, runs into a cash flow shortfall. In these early years, NEST is running a slightly higher shortfall than expected because the income levels of members are lower than expected.

Appendix III: Description of Selected National Legislative Efforts to Expand Workplace Retirement Savings Program Coverage Identified by GAO

To provide federal context, we interviewed federal agency officials and knowledgeable industry representatives, and we conducted targeted searches of legislative databases. Then from all bills in the 113th Congress and the 114th Congress categorized in the Legislative Information System as having retirement as a topic, we selected and discuss in the table below those that would make or would have made efforts to expand coverage in workplace retirement savings programs (see table 7). Because this is a select list, however, and we did not include bills that may have had an indirect effect on workplace retirement savings program coverage, this list should not be viewed as exhaustive.

Table 7. Description of Key Features of Selected Federal Legislative Proposals to Expand Workplace Retirement Savings Program Coverage

	Bill Title	Status	Description of Key Features
1	Automatic IRA Act of 2015 (S. 245 & H.R. 506)	Referred to Committees	The bill would, among other things, require eligible employers that do not maintain a qualifying plan or arrangement to make an automatic Individual Retirement Account (IRA) arrangement available to qualifying employees. Employers with no more than 10 employees or not in existence during the current and preceding calendar years would be excluded from the requirement. A tax is imposed on covered employers that do not meet the requirement. Generally, qualifying employees would be automatically enrolled to contribute 2 to 6 percent of their compensation, but may opt out. Complying employers with no more than 100 employees are eligible to receive a credit for maintaining automatic IRA arrangements.

Table 7. (Continued)

	Bill Title	Status	Description of Key Features
			To eliminate barriers to the use of multiple employer plans, the bill would also require the Departments of the Treasury and Labor to prescribe administrative guidance on several issues related to sponsorship of a plan by multiple employers.
			In 2013, a similar bill (H.R. 2035) was introduced and referred to committee but not enacted.
2	Retirement Security Act of 2015 (S. 266 & H.R. 557)	Referred to Committees	To eliminate a disincentive to pooling plan assets for multiple employer plans, among other things, this bill would require Treasury to prescribe regulations under which plans sponsored by multiple employers could be treated as qualified and modify the Employee Retirement Income Security Act of 1974 (ERISA) so that employers without a common interest could sponsor multiple employer plans. The bill would take other steps to expand coverage, such as allowing individuals to claim the Saver's Credit on the Internal Revenue Service Form 1040EZ.a
			In 2014, similar bills (S. 1970 &H.R. 4376) were introduced and referred to committees but were not enacted.
3	USA Retirement Funds Act (2014) (S. 1979 & H.R. 5818)	Not enacted	Among other things, this bill would have required employers that do not maintain a qualifying plan or arrangement to make an automatic USA Retirement Fund arrangement available to qualifying employees. Employers with no more than 10 employees or not in existence during the current and preceding calendar year would have been excluded from the requirement.

	Bill Title	Status	Description of Key Features
			Covered employers that did not meet this requirement would have been subject to civil monetary penalties. Generally, qualifying employees would have been automatically enrolled to contribute 3 percent of compensation in 2015 (increasing to 6 percent in 2018) to any qualified USA Retirement Fund, but would have been allowed to opt out or receive their contributions directly in cash. USA Retirement Funds would have been trust funds meeting specified requirements and publicly listed online, and employers would also have been permitted to make contributions to their employees' accounts, subject to limits. The bill would have also amended ERISA to provide that pooled employer plans, defined as a pension plan established or maintained by 2 or more employers, would have been treated as a single plan without regard to whether the employers involved had a common interest.
4	Small Businesses Add Value for Employees Act of 2014 or SAVE Act of 2014 (H.R. 5875)	Not enacted	This bill would have, among other things, authorized automatic deferral IRAs, under which employees who earned at least $5,000 the preceding year would have been automatically enrolled to contribute 3 percent of compensation to an IRA in the employee's first plan year (increasing to 15 percent in the 12th). It would have also increased the tax credit for small employer pension plan startup costs, and required outreach to and financial education of small businesses about the types and benefits of available retirement plans. The bill would have also provided that multiple employer plans established by employers without a common interest would have been treated as single plans.

Table 7. (Continued)

	Bill Title	Status	Description of Key Features
5	Secure Annuities for Employee Retirement Act of 2013 or SAFE Retirement Act of 2013 (S. 1270)	Not enacted	Among other things, this bill would have authorized a new retirement savings option called Starter 401(k) Deferral-Only Plans and allowed eligible employers not otherwise offering a qualified plan to sponsor them for eligible employees. Such plans would have had to include automatic enrollment and contributions from 3 to 15 percent of compensation up to $8,000, but employees could opt out. The legislation would have simplified reporting requirements for Starter 401(k) Plans and would not have treated them as top-heavy plans. The bill would have also provided that multiple employer plans established by employers without a common interest, but essentially operated by non-employers, serving as a designated plan providers, would have been treated as single employer plans.
6	Retirement Plan Simplification and Enhancement Act of 2013 (H.R. 2117)	Not enacted	This bill would have, among other things, modified and expanded the Saver's Credit. In addition, to encourage small employers to offer plans, the bill would have increased the tax credit for such employers when they start a pension plan or IRAs for employees. It would also have eliminated certain barriers to the use of multiple employer plans.
7	Savings for American Families' Future Act of 2013 (H.R. 837)	Not enacted	The bill would have expanded the availability of the Saver's Credit by increasing the rate of tax credit for retirement contributions, making it refundable, and directing Treasury to make, in effect, matching contributions.

Source: GAO review of legislative materials as of July 10, 2015. | GAO-15-556.

[a] Federal law authorizes a nonrefundable credit (the Saver's Credit) against federal income tax of up to $2,000 based on income for contributions to employee benefits plans or IRAs, with the credit phasing out entirely at certain income levels. 26 U.S.C. § 25B.

APPENDIX IV: DESCRIPTION OF STATE EFFORTS TO EXPAND WORKPLACE RETIREMENT SAVINGS PROGRAM COVERAGE IDENTIFIED BY GAO

We developed the following list of 29 states with recent efforts to expand retirement savings program coverage for private sector workers[1]— including the introduction, action on or enactment of legislation, an executive action, or a study—by (1) reviewing information posted online by industry stakeholders, including the National Council of State Legislatures, the Pension Rights Center, and other industry publications; (2) conducting targeted searches of enacted and proposed state legislation using LexisNexis and WestLaw, in consultation with a law librarian;[2] and (3) interviewing federal officials and knowledgeable industry representatives, including stakeholders at the Pension Rights Center, the American Society of Pension Professionals and Actuaries, and AARP. At multiple points during this process, we confirmed completeness of our list of states with knowledgeable industry stakeholders, including a more in-depth review by a representative of the Center for Retirement Initiatives at Georgetown University, a public policy center created to promote retirement savings solutions at the state level in the United States. (See fig. 11.)

We described the strategies proposed in the state efforts based on documentation we obtained from state legislative or executive office websites. We use "state efforts" to refer to a range of activities that may have occurred in a state, including the introduction of a bill, executive action, studies, or the enactment of legislation. While states are exploring various approaches, a number of state efforts seem to incorporate strategies, such as payroll deduction individual retirement accounts (IRAs) and automatic enrollment, that are similar to those incorporated into "automatic IRA" proposals submitted by the President and some members of Congress. We compiled this list, shown in table 8, by interviewing state officials and knowledgeable industry representatives and conducting targeted searches of legislative databases. We did not conduct an independent, legal analysis to determine whether the features and strategies used by states will hold up under scrutiny and this list may unintentionally exclude relevant state efforts that we did not identify.

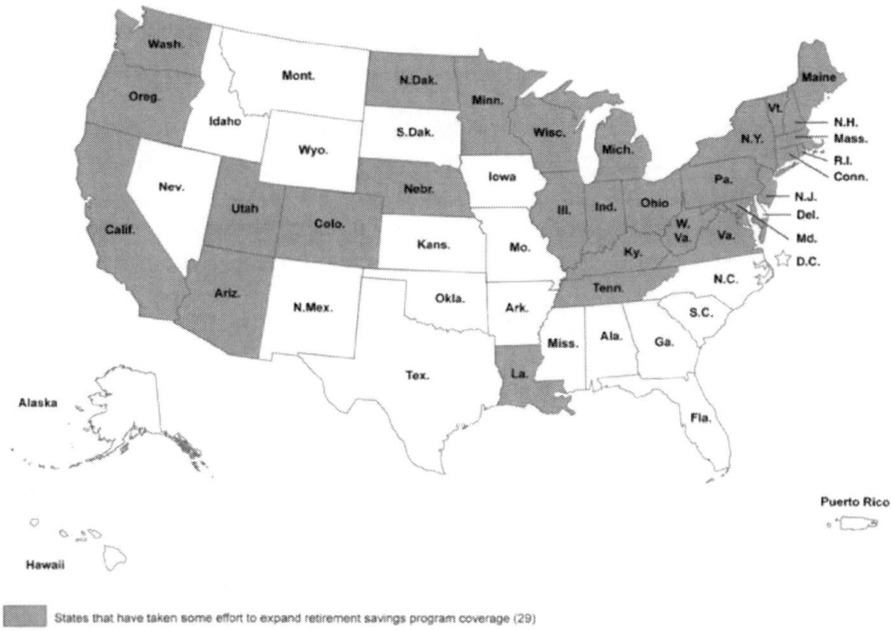

Source: GAO analysis of state legislative records and documentation, and testimonial evidence from knowledgeable industry representatives; Map Resources (map). | GAO-15-556.

Figure 11. States GAO Identified as Taking Some Effort to Expand Coverage in Workplace Retirement Savings Programs.

Table 8. Description of State Efforts to Increase Coverage of Workplace Retirement Savings Programs Identified by GAO

	State	Status	Description
1	Arizona	Not enacted	A bill introduced in 2014 would have required certain employers to automatically enroll their employees in a payroll deduction Individual Retirement Account (IRA) as part of the Arizona Secure Choice Retirement Savings Program.
2	California	Enacted	2012 law established the California Secure Choice Retirement Savings Program and Investment Board.

	State	Status	Description
			Under the program, eligible employers with 5 or more employees will be required to automatically enroll employees in a payroll deduction IRA. Prior to implementation of this program, the board is required to conduct a market analysis to determine whether the necessary conditions for implementation of the law could be met. The board has awarded contracts for (1) legal services, and (2) market analysis, feasibility study, and program design consultant services. A final report is expected no later than January 2016. The board is prohibited from opening the program for enrollment without a subsequent authorizing law.
		Not enacted	Bills to expand retirement savings coverage among private sector workers were introduced in 2008 and 2009. These proposals would have requested California's Public Employees Retirement System offer one or more IRAs, defined benefit plans, or multiple employer plans to eligible employees of participating private sector employers.
3	Colorado	Not enacted	Bills to create a Colorado retirement security task force were introduced in 2014 and 2015. The 2014 bill would have provided that the task force develop recommendations for increasing the percentage of Coloradans who are enrolled in a retirement plan which provides for a secure retirement. The 2015 bill would have provided that the task force study, assess, and report on the (1) factors that affect Coloradans' ability to save for a financially secure retirement and (2) feasibility of creating a retirement savings plan for private sector workers.

Table 8. (Continued)

	State	Status	Description
4	Connecticut	Enacted	In June 2014, legislation established the Connecticut Retirement Security Board to conduct a market feasibility study regarding the implementation of the public retirement plan for private sector workers and to develop a comprehensive proposal for the implementation of such a plan. The board is to report to the governor and a legislative committee on the results of the market feasibility study by January 1, 2016, and then develop a comprehensive proposal for the implementation of the public retirement plan.
		Not enacted	Several other bills to expand retirement plan coverage among private sector workers were introduced between 2009 and 2014. One bill would have established a voluntary defined contribution plan for small employers and charitable organizations, and another would have required qualified employers to automatically enroll their employees in payroll deduction IRAs.
5	Illinois	Enacted	A 2015 law created the Illinois Secure Choice Savings Program and Board. Under the program, eligible employers with 25 or more employees would be required to automatically enroll employees in a payroll deduction IRA. The program went into effect on June 1, 2015 and enrollment of employees is to begin before June 1, 2017 unless the board does not obtain adequate funding to implement the program.
		Not enacted	Several other bills to expand retirement plan coverage among private sector workers were introduced between 2011 and 2014.

	State	Status	Description
6	Indiana	Not enacted	A bill was introduced in 2015 that would have established the Hoosier Employee Retirement Option Plan, which would have maintained IRAs for employees of eligible employers voluntarily choosing to provide payroll deduction. In addition, bills proposed in 2013 and 2014 would have established a state-assisted retirement plan to encourage Indiana residents to increase their rate of savings and to build assets for use after retirement. Employer and employee participation would have been completely voluntary. In addition, the 2014 bill would have provided a one-time tax-credit for workers who participate in the state-assisted retirement plan.
7	Kentucky	Not enacted	In 2015, a bill was introduced that would have required certain employers to automatically enroll their employees into a payroll deduction IRA, called a Kentucky retirement account.
8	Louisiana	Not enacted	In 2014, a bill was introduced that would have required certain employers to automatically enroll their employees into the Louisiana Retirement Savings Plan.
9	Maine	Not enacted	A bill was introduced in 2015 that would have required certain employers to automatically enroll their employees in a payroll deduction IRA as part of a Maine Secure Choice Retirement Savings Program. A bill that would have established a similar program was introduced in 2013.
10	Maryland	Established	In 2014, Maryland's governor established a task force to ensure retirement security for all Marylanders. The task force issued a report in February 2015 that catalogued a range of possible proposals, and principles that should be considered in judging them, and strongly urged the state to develop and enact a program.[a]

Table 8. (Continued)

	State	Status	Description
		Not enacted	A bill was introduced in 2015 that would have established the Maryland Secure Choice Retirement Savings Program and Trust. This program would have required eligible employers with 5 or more employees to automatically enroll employees in a payroll deduction IRA. In addition, employers would have been able to voluntarily contribute to a profit sharing defined contribution plan for their employees. Several bills to expand retirement savings plan coverage for private sector workers were introduced between 2006and 2014. One bill would have established a voluntary plan for private sector employers to offer, and another would have required eligible employers to automatically enroll their employees in payroll deduction IRAs.
11	Massachusetts	Pending	Several bills to expand retirement savings plan coverage for private sector workers were introduced in 2015. One would create the Secure Choice Retirement Savings Plan and require eligible employers with 10 or more employees to (1) establish an employee benefit plan, (2) participate in a multiple employer plan created by the state, or (3) automatically enroll eligible employees into an IRA plan created by the state. The other bills would create the Massachusetts voluntary retirement accounts program that could include SIMPLE IRAs or workplace-based IRAs or a state-run defined contribution plan.

	State	Status	Description
		Enacted	A 2012 law authorized the state to sponsor a defined contribution plan that could be adopted by not-for-profit employers with 20 or fewer employees. As of June 2015, a state official noted that the plan was awaiting a determination letter from the Internal Revenue Service.
		Not enacted	A bill was introduced in 2011 that would have established the Massachusetts voluntary retirement accounts program under which employers would have been required to deduct and remit contributions from payroll upon request by workers. A bill in 2009 would have authorized a program that not-for-profit employers could offer their employees.
12	Michigan	Not enacted	A bill was introduced in 2007 that would have created an employee benefit plan administered by the state. Employer and employee participation would have been voluntary, and employers would have been able to contribute to workers' accounts.
13	Minnesota	Enacted	A 2014 law required the Minnesota Commissioner of Management and Budget to report on the potential for a state-administered retirement savings plan for workers without access to certain programs through their employer. $400,000 was appropriated for the report, and it was due Jan. 15, 2015. The state submitted a request for proposals in December 2014, but as of June 2015 a final report had not been released.
14	Nebraska	Completed	A 2013 legislative resolution asked the Nebraska Retirement Systems Committee to conduct an interim study related to the availability and adequacy of retirement savings of Nebraska private sector workers.

Table 8. (Continued)

	State	Status	Description
			This study resolution was referred to the executive committee in a May 2013 floor debate and on Dec. 10, 2013, the Nebraska Retirement Systems Committee held a public hearing on this topic.
15	New Hampshire	Not enacted	A bill was introduced in 2015 that would have established a statutory Commission on Retirement Security to study the creation of a retirement security program, and would have appropriated $100,000 to support the commission.
16	New Jersey	Pending	A bill was introduced in 2015 that would establish the New Jersey Secure Choice Savings Program Act, under which certain employers with 25 or more employees would be required to automatically enroll their employees into a payroll deduction IRA.
17	New York	Not enacted	A bill was introduced in 2011 that would have directed the Department of Audit and Control to examine, evaluate, and make recommendations regarding the establishment and operation of a public retirement system for employees of private providers of mental hygiene services.
18	North Dakota	Not enacted	A bill was introduced in 2015 that would have required the state Treasurer to establish a program that certain nongovernmental employers with 100 or fewer employees may have offered to their employees. Generally employee participation, as well as employer participation and contributions, would have been voluntary.
19	Ohio	Not enacted	A bill was introduced in 2013 that would have created the Ohio Secure Choice Retirement Savings Program under which certain employers with 20 or more employees would be required to automatically enroll their employees into the program.

	State	Status	Description
20	Oregon	Enacted	A 2015 law established the Oregon Retirement Savings Board, which will develop a defined contribution retirement plan for Oregon workers and conduct a market and legal analysis of the plan. Among other things the plan must provide for automatic enrollment and requires employers to offer their employees an opportunity to contribute to the plan unless the employers offer a qualified retirement plan. Also, a 2013 law established the Oregon Retirement Savings Task Force to develop and report recommendations for increasing the percentage of Oregonians saving for retirement or enrolled in a retirement plan, and for increasing the amount of those individual savings. The task force report, issued in 2014, recommended developing and making available a retirement savings plan with a minimal employer role, automatic enrollment for the employee, and payroll deduction, among other things.[b]
21	Pennsylvania	Not enacted	A bill was introduced in 2007 that would have directed the state treasurer to establish a bureau within the department to establish and administer the Pennsylvania Voluntary Accounts Program, which would have maintained accounts for eligible employees of certain private-sector employers voluntarily choosing to provide access to the program.
22	Rhode Island	Enacted	Joint resolutions in 2009 and 2010 established a special legislative commission to study the establishment of Universal Voluntary Retirement Accounts.
23	Tennessee	Enacted	A 2008 joint resolution instructed the state treasurer to study and, by Feb.1, 2009, report on the feasibility of establishing a voluntary retirement plan for small businesses in

Table 8. (Continued)

	State	Status	Description
			Tennessee that would offer 401(k) plans and other savings vehicles. The treasurer found that encouraging employers to implement a plan is worthwhile, but putting the state in the middle of this process could actually increase costs, so it did not make any recommendations for state action.[c]
24	Utah	Enrolled	A 2015 joint resolution strongly urged Utah's small business employees and its small business community to join with the Legislature and the Utah treasurer to study and develop a model for saving for retirement through the workplace that is accessible to the workers of Utah and consider legislation, if needed, to put the plan into action. A 2014 joint resolution determined that certain legislative issues required additional study, including how to help people prepare to be financially self-sufficient in retirement.
25	Vermont	Enacted	A 2014 law created a Public Retirement Plan Study Committee to evaluate the feasibility of establishing a public retirement plan and, if it determines that such a plan is necessary, feasible, and effective, to also study how to ensure that the plan is available to private sector employees who are not covered by an alternative retirement plan. On Jan. 15, 2015, the Public Retirement Plan Study Committee released a report recommending further study.[d]
26	Virginia	Enacted	A 2015 law directed the Virginia Retirement System to convene a work group to review current state and federal programs that encourage citizens of the Commonwealth to save for retirement, including an

	State	Status	Description
			examination of the retirement savings options for self-employed individuals, part-time employees, full-time employees whose employers do not offer a retirement savings plan, and groups with a low savings rate. A report of the work group's findings is due by Jan. 1, 2017.
		Not enacted	2009 legislation would have established the Virginia Employee Voluntary Accounts Program to enhance the accessibility and affordability of payroll savings deduction plans for small employers and their employees to voluntarily participate.
27	Washington	Enacted	A 2015 law established the Washington small business retirement marketplace to connect eligible employers with fewer than 100 employees and their employees with approved plans that, among other things, do not charge employers administrative fees and charge workers 1 percent of their account balance or less in total annual fees. Participation is voluntary for employers and employees. Also, pursuant to legislation enacted in 2007, officials issued a report identifying three options for a state sponsored retirement program for private sector workers.[e]
		Not enacted	Several other bills to expand retirement plan coverage among private sector workers were introduced between 2007 and 2014.
28	West Virginia	Enacted	A resolution was introduced in 2008 to study the benefits, costs and feasibility of establishing a West Virginia Universal Voluntary Accounts Program to assist private employers in offering employees an optional retirement plan. The state treasurer's office established a working group and drafted new legislation.

Table 8. (Continued)

	State	Status	Description
		Not enacted	A 2015 Senate concurrent resolution would have requested the Joint Committee on Government and Finance to study the need and feasibility of the state creating a cost-effective and portable group retirement savings program for small businesses—fewer than 50 employees—and their employees. Several other bills and one resolution were introduced between 2009 and 2014 that would have created the West Virginia Voluntary Employee Retirement Account(s) Program or requested a study on such a program.
29	Wisconsin	Pending	A bill introduced in 2015 would create a Wisconsin private retirement security board that would study the feasibility of establishing a private security retirement plan for private-sector workers, design a plan, and submit a report to the legislature.
		Not enacted	A bill was introduced in 2014 that would have had provisions similar to those proposed in 2015.

Source: GAO analysis of state legislative records and documentation, and testimonial evidence from knowledgeable industry representatives, as of July 28, 2015. | GAO-15-556

[a] Governor's Task Force to Ensure Retirement Security for All Marylanders. *1,000,000 of Our Neighbors at Risk: Improving Retirement Security for Marylanders.* February 2015.

[b] Oregon Retirement Savings Task Force. *Report and Recommendations of the Oregon Retirement Savings Task Force Created and Tasked Pursuant to HB 3436 (2013).* Sept. 15, 2014.

[c] Tennessee Treasurer. *SJR 1075 Feasibility Study Report: State Sponsored Small Business Retirement Savings Plan.*

[d] State of Vermont, Office of the State Treasurer. *Interim Study of the Feasibility of Establishing a Public Retirement Plan Required by Section C. 108 of Act 179 of 2014.*

[e] Washington State Department of Retirement Systems. *Washington Voluntary Accounts: Report to the Legislature* January 2009.

APPENDIX V

Canada

At a Glance

Access to workplace retirement plans has declined in Canada and government officials and stakeholders reported that middle income workers, in particular, were not adequately prepared for retirement. According to a recent industry report, about 17 percent of Canadian households are not adequately prepared for retirement. To address this gap, the federal government passed the Pooled Registered Pension Plans (PRPP) Act in 2012, which created defined contribution plans that federally regulated employers can choose to offer their workers. The federal PRPP Act covers PRPPs offered to workers in specific industries, such as banking or inter-provincial transportation, and those workers who are employed or self-employed in the Canadian territories. Some provinces are in various stages of planning and implementation of their own PRPP legislation for provincially regulated employers. For example, Quebec's version of PRPPs, the Voluntary Retirement Savings Plan (VRSP), took effect in July 2014, and is being phased in over 4 years starting with large employers, with the rollout scheduled to be complete by 2018.

According to research by a Canadian financial institution, VRSP is estimated to enroll 1 million workers in the province by 2018. Because the PRPP is voluntary for employers and implementation is in the early stages, estimates on participation rates remain unclear.

Source: GAO analysis of foreign agency documentation and interviews with Canadian officials and industry experts.

Workplace Access and Automatic Enrollment

Federally regulated and most provincially regulated employers can voluntarily offer PRPPs to their workers, while Quebec will require employers with five or more eligible workers to offer VRSP. If a federally or provincially regulated employer chooses to offer a PRPP, or is required to offer VRSP, the employer will contract with a licensed provider who will manage the set-up process. Eligible workers will be automatically enrolled. However, workers have 60 days to opt out or may, 12 months after their contributions begin, set their contribution rate to zero for a fixed period of up to five years. Full-time workers are immediately eligible to join a PRPP and part-time workers are eligible after 24 months of continuous service. Eligible workers for Quebec's VRSP are those who are ages 18 and older, have 1 year of continuous service, and who otherwise do not have the opportunity to contribute to a workplace retirement plan.

Financial Incentives and Worker Contributions

PRPPs and VRSPs offer workers tax benefits to encourage participation, but contribution requirements vary. Worker contributions to PRPP receive a corresponding tax deduction up to a set contribution limit. Default contribution rates will be set by the plan administrator for their PRPP, but providers may permit workers to adjust the contribution rate. For VRSP, the default contribution rate is set by regulation at 2 percent until 2017, increasing to 3 percent in 2018 and 4 percent in 2019. However, workers can alternatively set their contribution rate to zero. Employers are not required to make financial contributions to their workers PRPP or VRSP accounts.

Plan Providers

Service providers, like banks or insurance companies, must apply for a license to become an administrator of PRPPs or VRSPs, and take on the fiduciary responsibility for administering the plans.

Investment Options

Licensed administrators will offer a limited number of investment options including a default option that will be either a balanced fund or a target date fund, and up to five additional investment options with varying degrees of risk.

Fees

To ensure fees are reasonable, government regulation requires that PRPP providers charge fees equivalent to or below those charged to members of defined contribution plans with 500 or more members. As of July 2015, VRSP fees for the default option range between 1.09 and 1.25 percent.

New Zealand

> **At a glance**
>
> To increase national savings and address the declining trend in private sector retirement plan coverage of the under 65 population—from about 20 percent in 2001 to about 15 percent in 2007—the New Zealand government passed the KiwiSaver Act. The act established KiwiSaver in 2007 as a government-sponsored defined contribution workplace program. KiwiSaver requires employers to automatically enroll all new workers into a qualified plan, with a worker opt-out. Workers are encouraged to participate in KiwiSaver through a series of incentives that include employer contributions, tax benefits, and a one-time government contribution.
>
> As of June 2014, KiwiSaver had grown to include 2.35 million members. Of this total, approximately 61 percent chose to opt into KiwiSaver either through their employer or through a plan provider. The remaining 39 percent were automatically enrolled by their employer. Approximately 20 percent of enrolled workers have chosen to opt out of KiwiSaver.
>
> Source: GAO analysis of foreign agency documentation and interviews with New Zealand officials and industry experts.

Workplace Access and Automatic Enrollment

Employers are required to automatically enroll new workers ages 18 to 65 into a KiwiSaver plan. In addition, existing workers, as well as the self-employed and unemployed, can choose to opt into a KiwiSaver plan by notifying their employer or by contacting a provider directly. Employers can select a preferred provider for workers who do not choose their own, but workers have the right to change providers anytime. Following automatic enrollment, workers have between 2 and 8 weeks to opt out.

Financial Incentives and Worker Contributions

Participation in KiwiSaver offers eligible workers employer contributions, tax benefits, and a one-time government contribution, to complement workers' own contributions. For workers who do not opt out, employers are generally required to contribute 3 percent of earnings. In addition, workers who contribute a minimum of $1,043 New Zealand dollars (NZD) (about $663

USD) or more annually get a $521 NZD ($331 USD) tax credit. Until May 21, 2015, the government also made a one-time kick start contribution of $1,000 for new accounts. After this date, new members are no longer eligible for this payment. Workers generally contribute 3, 4, or 8 percent of earnings. After an initial 12 month period, workers have the option of a contributions holiday from 3 months to 5 years.

Plan Providers

KiwiSaver service providers, such as banks, insurance companies and investment firms, are registered to offer qualifying plans, and deal directly with workers after the initial set-up process. If an employer does not have a preferred KiwiSaver provider and a worker does not select one, Inland Revenue, the government tax collection and social programs agency, allocates workers to one of the nine government-appointed default service providers. All service providers are registered with and monitored by the Financial Markets Authority, the government regulator.

Investment Options

KiwiSaver service providers offer a range of products with different investment options and risk levels with the default being a conservatively invested fund. Approximately 25 percent of KiwiSaver participants are in a default investment fund.

Fees

Default service providers are licensed by Inland Revenue and establish reasonable fees for participants by submitting a fee schedule as part of the application process. Inland Revenue must also approve any changes to the fee structure. In addition, the Commission for Financial Capability established Fund Finder, an online tool that allows participants to compare plan features and fee structures. Over half of KiwiSaver plans charge between 1 and 1.5 percent in fees—New Zealand uses a Total Expense Ratio tool to measure fees, which is a ratio of total fees to funds under management in percentage terms.

United Kingdom

At a glance

To address the declining proportion of private sector workers participating in a workplace retirement plan—down from 47 percent in 2002 to about 32 percent in 2012—the United Kingdom government passed legislation in 2008 requiring employers to automatically enroll all eligible workers into a retirement plan. Employers can meet their obligation by enrolling workers in a plan that meets minimum standards or the new National Employment Savings Trust (NEST) set up by the government.

Automatic enrollment is being phased in over the course of several years beginning with the largest employers. Since its implementation began, the rollout had reached over 50,000 employers and 5.3 million workers by end of June 2015. An additional 1.2 million employers are scheduled to implement automatic enrollment for approximately 4 million employees by April 2017. The rollout is scheduled to be completed by 2018, when it will cover employers of all sizes. Worker opt-out rates were approximately 9 to 10 percent in 2013 and 12 percent in 2014, below the initial government estimates of 33 percent.

Source: GAO analysis of foreign agency documentation and interviews with United Kingdom officials and industry experts.

Workplace Access and Automatic Enrollment

Employers are required to automatically enroll workers to a qualified workplace retirement plan if they are between age 22 and State Pension Age—which is variable based on age, gender, years of employment, and national insurance status—and have earnings over 10,000 British pounds (GBP) (about $15,353 USD) for the 2015/2016 tax year. The U.K. government reviews the threshold annually and may adjust it. Once they have been automatically enrolled, workers have 1 month to opt out. Some workers earning less than 10,000 GBP, ages 16 to 21, and over the State Pension Age have the option to opt in. Every 3 years, employers are required to automatically re-enroll workers who have previously opted out.

Financial Incentives and Worker Contributions

For workers who do not opt out, the total minimum contribution from the employer, government, and worker will combine to reach 8 percent by 2018. Employers are required to contribute 1 percent of qualified earnings—a band of earnings between 5,824 GBP and 42,385 GBP (about $8,941 USD and $65,073 USD) as of 2015—gradually increasing to 3 percent by 2018. In addition, the U.K. government will contribute the equivalent of 1 percent of qualified earnings in the form of tax relief by that date. Workers currently pay 0.8 percent of qualified earnings, gradually increasing to 4 percent by 2018, through payroll deduction.

Plan Providers

Employers may offer a plan through a commercial provider, such as an insurance company, if it meets or exceeds certain legal criteria. If an employer does not offer a qualifying plan, they must enroll workers into NEST, which was established to act as a low-cost default provider. It has a public service obligation to accept any employer that wants to use it, including smaller employers that may not be able to find suitable commercial providers.

Investment Options

NEST offers a limited number of investment options to reduce complexity and fees. The default fund is a diversified target date fund, which is conservatively invested to avoid capital loss during initial years of saving to discourage workers from opting out. In addition to the default, NEST offers five other options with varying levels of risk.

Fees

NEST does not charge employers to use the program. Workers enrolled in NEST pay an annual management fee of 0.3 percent. A temporary additional fee of 1.8 percent on contributions is also deducted until NEST start-up costs are recovered. According to NEST officials, this is equivalent to a total fee of about 0.5 percent annually, which is comparable to fees charged by larger workplace retirement programs. From April 2015 onward, workers who enroll with non-NEST commercial providers pay an annual charge fee capped at 0.75 percent.

APPENDIX VI: TECHNICAL APPENDIX FOR DATA ANALYSIS

Factors Affecting Workplace Retirement Program Participation

In this appendix we summarize the results of our analyses of factors affecting retirement program participation. We first looked at the likelihood of participating in retirement programs overall, or among all workers. We then examined, among all workers, the likelihood of their employers offering them retirement programs. Then, among workers whose employers offered programs, we looked at the likelihoods of workers being eligible for them. And finally, we looked at the likelihood of participating in retirement programs among workers who were offered programs and eligible for them. In all of these analyses, we estimated how these different likelihoods were associated with different characteristics of the workers, including their income, occupation, education, age, gender, marital status, race/ethnicity, the size of the firm they worked for, whether they worked full-time or part-time, whether they worked for the full year or only part of the year, and whether they were or were not union members.

For our analyses, we used publicly available data from the Survey of Income and Program Participation (SIPP) from 2012, as shown in tables 9 – 12 of this appendix. To correct for under-reporting of participation we also used W-2 data as described in appendix I. Results from the public use data and W-2 data were very similar in the size and significance of variables included in our analysis, as shown in table 13 at the end of this appendix. In all of the tables, the numbers and estimates derived from them use weighted data to reflect population estimates, using weights provided by SIPP.

Likelihood of Participating

Table 9 shows how various categories of workers differ in their likelihood (expressed both as percentages and odds) of participating in retirement programs. In the first column of numbers in the table we show the number of workers in each group (or category) defined by the different factors. The next two columns of numbers reflect the percentages in each group that were and were not participating in retirement programs. The traditional way of comparing groups involves considering the difference in those percentages, and those differences are in many cases quite sizable. For example, only 14 percent of the workers in the lowest income quartile were participating in retirement programs, while 76 percent of the workers in the highest income quartile were participating in retirement programs. Only 18 percent of workers with less than a high school diploma, but 62 percent of workers with at least a bachelor's degree, were participating in retirement programs. And while only 23 percent of the workers in firms with fewer than 50 workers were participating in retirement programs, 60 percent of workers in firms with more than 1,000 workers were retirement program participants. Sizable differences also exist between most of the categories of workers defined by the other characteristics shown in the table.

Odds and Odds Ratios

An alternative method of estimating the likelihood of participating in retirement programs and the differences in those likelihoods between groups involves calculating odds and odds ratios. The odds on participating (vs. not participating) in retirement programs are calculated by taking, overall or for any one group, the number (or percent) of workers participating in retirement programs and dividing it by the number (or percent) of workers not participating in retirement programs. Overall, using the percentages in the final row of table 9, the odds on participating in retirement programs in our (weighted) sample of workers is 45.4 ÷ 54.6 = .832, apart from rounding.[1] While somewhat different and less traditional than percentages, the odds have a fairly direct and simple interpretation: In this case it implies that overall there are .83 retirement program participants for every 1 non-participant, or 83 participants for every 100 non-participants. In the fourth column of numbers in table 9, we show the odds on participating for each subgroup defined by the different worker characteristics shown in the table. There we see, for example, that the odds on participating in retirement programs increases from 0.167 for workers in the lowest income quartile to 0.514 for workers in the second income quartile to 1.338 for workers in the third income quartile and, finally, to 3.176 for workers in the highest income quartile.

The unadjusted odds ratios in the penultimate column of table 9 show how the odds on participating in retirement programs vary across the different subgroups. Where the factors or worker characteristics distinguish only two groups, like union membership, we simply take the ratio of the odds for one group to the other – e.g., 2.103 ÷ 0.774 = 2.72, which implies that the odds on union members participating in retirement programs are 2.7 times higher than the odds for workers who are not union members. Where the factors involve more than two subgroups, we choose one subgroup as the referent category and calculated the ratios of the odds for the other subgroups relative to that one. To make comparisons across income categories, for example, the lowest income quartile was chosen as the referent category, and the ratios shown for the other subgroups (i.e., 0.514 ÷ 0.167 = 3.08; 1.338 ÷ 0.167 = 8.01; and 3.176 ÷ 0.167 = 19.01) indicate that workers in the second, third, and highest income quartiles have higher odds on participating than workers in the lowest quartile, by factors of 3, 8, and 19, respectively. The full set of unadjusted odds ratios shown in the table indicate that virtually all of the subgroups differ from one another, in most cases significantly, and in many cases by a substantively large amount.[2] Workers in the broad category of occupations involving Management, Business, Science, and Arts, for example, were 6.5 times as likely to be participating in retirement plans (or have odds that are 6.5 times higher) as workers working in Service occupations. Workers with bachelor's degrees were 2.7 times as likely as workers with less than a high school education to be participating in retirement programs. And, to offer a final example, Hispanics were less likely than white non-Hispanics to be participating in a retirement program by a factor of 0.37.

These unadjusted odds ratios may seem to inflate the differences between groups, especially to those who are accustomed to comparing percentages. That is, while the odds ratio comparing workers in the highest and lowest income quartiles suggests a 19-fold difference between the two groups, there is only slightly more than a 5-fold difference between the two groups in the percentage participating (i.e., 76.1 ÷ 14.3 = 5.3). Focusing on the difference between groups in the percent participating, however, ignores the implicit difference in the percent not participating between groups, which differed by a factor of 23.9 ÷ 85.7 = 0.28. One advantage of the odds ratio (also referred to as the cross-product ratio) is that in estimating the ratios of participants to non-participants it makes fuller use of the data involved in the comparisons, and considers both differences at once. In fact, the odds ratio we obtain in this case, equal to 19.01, could just as easily have been obtained by taking the ratio of these two percentage differences (i.e., 5.3 ÷ 0.28 = 19.01, apart from rounding).

Regression Results

Overall Participation

Another advantage of odds ratios is that, unlike percentage differences, they can be adjusted using multivariate models (logistic regression models) so that they reflect the net effect of each variable, rather than the gross (or unadjusted) effect. The odds ratios in the final column of table 9 show how different the odds on participating are when we consider all of the variables in the table simultaneously. Because of the correlations among some of the variables in the table (like income and education), the effects of the different variables, or the differences between the categories of workers they define, are in many cases substantially attenuated (or smaller) when we look at them simultaneously than when we look at each individually. The odds ratio estimating the income difference just discussed, for example, is reduced when we estimate its effect net of the other variables, from 19.0 to 6.8. Even after adjusting the ratios to take account of the interrelatedness of many of the factors in the table, most of the subgroups compared remain significantly different from one another, and in many cases the differences are sizable. In addition to the income difference mentioned above we find, even after adjustment, that the likelihood of participating varies significantly for many of the variables we examined (see table 9). For example:

1) Workers in all other occupational categories have significantly higher odds on participating in retirement programs than workers in Service occupations, and the odds are nearly twice as high (OR = 1.95) for workers in Management, Business, Science, and Arts occupations as for those in Service occupations.
2) Workers with less than a high school diploma were less likely (by a factor of 0.6) than those with less than a high school education to be participating, though after adjustment those with some college or with a Bachelor’s degree are not statistically distinguishable from those with a high school diploma.
3) Workers in larger firms had higher odds on participating in retirement programs than workers in smaller firms. Workers in firms with 51 to 100 workers were about twice as likely (OR = 2.1) as workers in firms with 50 or fewer workers to participate, and workers in firms with more than 1,000 workers were about five times (OR = 4.9) as likely.
4) The youngest category of workers (ages 18-24) were only roughly one-third as likely (OR =0.37) as workers 25-34 to be participating in retirement programs; workers 35-44 were not significantly different from workers 25-34; and workers 45-54 and 55-64 were both more likely than those 25-34 to be participating in retirement programs, in both cases by a factor of 1.4. Workers 65 and over had lower odds on

participating than all groups except the very youngest, and odds that were lower than workers 25-34 by a factor of 0.68.

5) Additionally, full-time workers were 1.6 times more likely than part-time workers to be participating in retirement programs; full-year workers were 2.5 times more likely than part-year workers to be participating in retirement programs; and union workers were twice as likely (OR = 2.0) as non-union workers to be participating in retirement plans.
6) Finally, male workers were less likely than female workers to be participating in retirement programs, by a factor of 0.91; currently married workers were 1.2 times more likely than never married workers to be participating in retirement programs, while widowed, divorced, and separated workers were not significantly different from those who were never married; and Black, Hispanic, and Asian workers had lower odds on participating than White, non-Hispanic workers, by factors of 0.8, 0.6, and 0.7, respectively.

Employer Offers Program

Some of these differences in the likelihood of participating in retirement programs are likely due to the fact that some categories of workers are more likely than others to work for employers that offer retirement programs. Table 10 shows that a great many categories of workers differ in terms of whether their employer offers a program. As in the table above, the unadjusted odds ratios indicating the differences between groups in the odds on their employers offering a program (in the penultimate column of the table) tend to be somewhat larger than the adjusted odds ratios, or the odds ratios obtained from multivariate models in which all of the different factors are considered simultaneously using a multivariate model (in the final column). But even the adjusted odds ratios reveal some sizable and significant differences, including the following:

1) Workers with higher incomes are more likely to work for employers that offer retirement programs. Workers in the 2nd, 3rd, and highest income quartiles have higher odds on working for employers that offer retirement programs than workers in the lowest income quartile, by factors of 1.7, 2.7, and 3.9, respectively.
2) Workers in all occupational categories except for Natural Resources, Construction, and Maintenance Occupations have significantly higher

odds on working for employers that offer retirement programs than workers in Service occupations, and the odds are nearly twice as high (OR = 2.0) for workers in Management, Business, Science, and Arts occupations as for those in Service occupations.

3) Workers with less than a high school education were less likely to work for employers that offer retirement programs than those with a high school diploma, by a factor of 0.73, while workers with some college or a Bachelor's degree were more likely (in both cases) by a factor of roughly 1.2.
4) Workers in larger firms had substantially higher odds on working for employers that offer retirement programs than workers in smaller firms. Workers in firms with 51 to 100 workers were about three times as likely (OR = 2.95) as workers in firms with 50 or fewer workers to work for employers that offer retirement programs, workers in firms with 101 to 500 workers and with 501 to 1,000 workers were 5 and 6 times as likely, respectively, and workers in firms with more than 1,000 workers were about 9 times (OR = 9.1) as likely to work for employers that offer retirement programs.
5) The youngest category of workers (ages18-24) were only roughly three-fourths as likely (OR =0.76) as workers 25-34 to be working for employers that offer retirement programs; workers 35-44 were also somewhat less likely than workers 25-34 to work for employers that offer retirement programs (OR = 0.88); and workers 45-54 and 55-64 did not significantly differ from those 25-34 in working for employers that offer retirement programs. Workers 65 and over had lower odds on working for employers that offer retirement programs than all groups, and odds that were lower than workers 18-24 by a factor of 0.62.
6) Additionally, full-time workers were 1.2 times more likely than part-time workers to be working for employers that offer retirement programs; full-year workers were 1.5 times more likely than part-year workers to be working for employers that offer retirement programs, and union workers were twice as likely (OR = 2.0) as non-union workers to be working for employers that offer retirement programs.
7) Finally, male workers and female workers did not significantly differ in their chance of working for employers that offer retirement programs (OR = 0.96); currently married workers were slightly but significantly (OR = 1.1) more likely than never married workers to be

working for employers that offer retirement programs, while widowed, divorced, and separated workers were not significantly different from those who were never married; and Black, Hispanic, and Asian workers had lower odds on working for employers that offer retirement programs than White, non-Hispanic workers, by factors of 0.8, 0.6, and 0.6, respectively.

Eligibility

Some of these differences in the likelihood of participating in retirement programs are also likely due to the fact that some categories of workers are more likely than others to be eligible for the retirement programs that their employers offer. Table 11 shows that a number of categories of workers differ in terms of whether they are eligible for the retirement programs their employers offer, though fewer factors are significantly associated with eligibility than participation. The differences that do exist, like those described above, are in virtually all cases somewhat smaller when we estimate them simultaneously than when we estimate them separately; nonetheless, the odds ratios from the multivariate models indicate that:

1) Workers with higher incomes are more likely to be eligible for the retirement programs their employers offer than workers with lower incomes. Workers in the 2nd, 3rd, and highest income quartiles have higher odds on being eligible than workers in the lowest quartile, by factors of 2.0, 4.4, and 7.5, respectively.
2) Occupation was not significantly associated with whether workers were eligible for the retirement programs their employers offer. Education was significantly related to eligibility, however; workers with some college and with a college degree were less likely than those with a high school degree to be eligible, by factors of 0.8 and 0.7, respectively.
3) Workers in mid-size firms were not significantly different from workers in the smallest firms in their chance of being eligible for the retirement programs their employers offer, though workers in firms with more than 1,000 workers were 1.3 times as likely to be eligible as workers in firms with 50 or fewer workers.
4) The youngest category of workers (ages 18-24) were less than one-half as likely (OR = 0.44) as workers 25-34 to be eligible for retirement programs their employers offer, while workers 35-44, 45-

54, and 55- 64 were more likely to be eligible than those 25-34, by factors of 1.4, 1.6, and 1.6, respectively. Workers 65 and over were less likely to be eligible than workers 18-24, by a factor of 0.73.

5) Full-time workers were 2.6 times more likely than part-time workers to be eligible for the retirement programs their employers offer; full-year workers were 3.1 times more likely than part-year workers to be eligible for the retirement programs their employers offer; and union workers were 1.4 as likely as non-union workers to be eligible for the retirement programs their employers offer.
6) 6. Finally, male workers and female workers did not significantly differ in their chance of being eligible for the retirement programs their employers offer (OR = 1.1); currently married workers were significantly more likely (OR = 1.4) than never married workers to be eligible for the retirement programs their employers offer, while widowed, divorced, and separated workers were not significantly different from those who were never married; and race and ethnicity was not significantly associated with eligibility.

Participation among Those Eligible

Given these results indicating that participation in retirement programs is partly the result of whether programs are offered, and whether workers are eligible for them, in table 12 we show how various categories of workers differ in their likelihood of participating in retirement programs when we restrict our attention to workers whose employers offer programs for which they are eligible. While differences are in most cases smaller than they appeared when we looked at all workers, regardless of whether they worked for companies that offered retirement programs and whether they were eligible for them, many still remain sizable and statistically significant. Focusing again on the multivariate odds ratios in the final column of the table, the results are as follows among those who were eligible for the programs their employers offered:

1) Workers with higher incomes are more likely to participate than workers with lower incomes. Workers in the 2nd, 3rd, and highest income quartiles have higher odds on participating in retirement programs than workers in the lowest income quartile, by factors of 1.2, 2.2, and 4.4, respectively.

2) Workers in all occupational categories except for Production, Transportation, and Material Moving Occupations have significantly higher odds on participating in retirement programs than workers in Service occupations, by factors ranging from 1.3 to 1.5.
3) Workers with less than a high school diploma were less likely (by a factor of 0.7) than those with a high school education to be participating, though after adjustment those with some college or with a Bachelor's degree are not significantly different from those with a high school diploma.
4) Workers in firms with 51 to 100 workers were somewhat less likely (OR = 0.75) as workers in firms with 50 or fewer workers to participate, while workers in each of the larger firm categories (with more than 100 workers) were not significantly different from the smallest firms.
5) The youngest category of workers (ages 18-24) were only roughly one-half as likely (OR =0.46) as workers 25-34 to be participating in retirement programs; workers 35-44, 45-54, and 55-64 were more likely than those 25-34 to be participating in retirement programs, by factors of 1.3, 1.7, and 1.9, respectively. Workers 65 and over had odds of participating that were not statistically distinguishable from the odds for workers 25-34 (OR = 0.9).
6) Full-time workers were slightly more likely (OR =1.1) than part-time workers to be participating in retirement programs; full-year workers were 1.3 times more likely than part-year workers to be participating in retirement programs, though the result was not statistically significant; and union workers were 1.7 times as likely as non-union workers to be participating in retirement programs.
7) Finally, male workers were less likely than female workers to be participating in retirement programs, by a factor of 0.8; marital status was not statistically associated with participation; and Black and Hispanic workers had lower odds on participating than White, non-Hispanic workers, by factors of roughly 0.7 in both cases. Asians and other non-Hispanics were not significantly different from Whites.

Ignoring for the moment the numbers in parentheses, table 13 summarizes how the differences in participating across groups change when we look at the different group characteristics (1) one at a time among all workers, (2) all at once among all workers, and (3) all at once among workers who are eligible for the retirement programs offered by their employers. Some of the differences that appear sizable and significant when we look at them in isolation (column 1) diminish in size and become insignificant when all of the different factors are considered simultaneously (column 2). This is true of the differences between 1) workers with more than a high school education vs. workers with only a high school diploma, 2) workers ages 35-44 vs. workers ages 25-34, 3) workers who are widowed, divorced, or separated vs. workers who were never married, and 4) other non-Hispanic workers and white non-Hispanic workers. Further, some of the differences that remain sizable and significant even when they are considered simultaneously (column 2) diminish and become insignificant when we restrict the sample to workers who were offered programs and were eligible for them (column 3). Such is the case with the differences between 1) workers in Production, Transportation, and Material Moving Occupations vs. workers in Service Occupations, 2) workers in each of the larger firm categories with more than 100 workers vs. those in firms with 50 or fewer workers, 3) workers 65 and older vs. workers 25-34, 4) full-year vs. part-year workers, 5) married vs. never married workers, and 6) Asian non-Hispanic vs. white non-Hispanic workers. Most of the differences that remain significant after taking account of eligibility, which are noted in the bullets above associated with table 12, are smaller than they appeared before taking account of eligibility, though some of the age differences are exceptions to this. The factors that have the most pronounced effects when they are considered jointly and restricted to eligible workers are income, occupation, age, and union membership.

The numbers in parentheses in the table show these same coefficients from the same bivariate and multivariate models for the same subgroups that we obtain when we use the "corrected" data which combines W-2 information from the Census with the self-reported data from SIPP. In virtually all cases the coefficients are very similar, and only in a few instances, involving the adjusted education effect for all workers, and the adjusted differences between part-time and full-time workers and workers in firms with 1,000+ workers and in firms with fewer than 50 workers among those who are eligible, are the estimated odds ratios significant in one set of results but not in the other. In virtually all other instances, the effects are similar in both size and significance.

Table 9. Percentages of Workers of Different Types Participating and Not Participating in Retirement Programs, and Odds and Odds Ratios Derived from Them

Variable	Category	Total	Participating	Not Participating	Odds on Participating	Odds Ratio	Odds Ratio (Multivariate)
Income	Lowest Quartile	25,569,365	14.3	85.7	0.167		
	2nd Quartile	25,493,645	33.9	66.1	0.514	3.08*	2.00*
	3rd Quartile	25,643,901	57.2	42.8	1.338	8.01*	4.04 *
	Highest Quartile	25,575,562	76.1	23.9	3.176	19.01*	6.84 *
Occupation	1. Management, Business, Science, and Arts Occupations	32,917,449	64.0	36.0	1.774	6.48 *	1.95*
	2. Service Occupations	18,465,079	21.5	78.5	0.274		
	3. Sales and Office Occupations	27,175,235	43.2	56.8	0.760	2.78*	1.54*
	4. Natural Resources, Construction, and Maintenance Occupations	9,619,204	37.9	62.1	0.610	2.23*	1.25*
	5. Production, Transportation, and Material Moving Occupations	14,105,504	42.8	57.2	0.749	2.74 *	1.44*
Education	1. LT HS Diploma	8,095,918	18.1	81.9	0.221	0.37*	0.61*
	2. HS Diploma	26,703,135	37.2	62.8	0.593		

Table 9. (Continued)

Variable	Category	Total	Participating	Not Participating	Odds on Participating	Odds Ratio	Odds Ratio (Multivariate)
	3. Some College	37,213,439	43.8	56.2	0.779	1.31*	1.03
	4. Bachelor's or More	30,269,980	61.9	38.1	1.625	2.74*	1.06
Firm Size	1. More Than 1,000 Workers	44,333,968	59.6	40.4	1.473	4.85*	4.93 *
	2. 501 to 1,000 Workers	4,822,085	54.0	46.0	1.175	3.87*	3.57 *
	3. 101 to 500 Workers	13,086,877	52.0	48.0	1.083	3.57*	3.01*
	4. 51 to 100 Workers	7,025,518	41.8	58.2	0.719	2.37*	2.07*
	5. 50 or Fewer Workers	33,014,024	23.3	76.7	0.304		
Age	Age2: 18 - 24	13,224,335	11.9	88.1	0.135	0.18*	0.37 *
	Age2: 25 - 34	24,119,413	43.1	56.9	0.757		
	Age2: 35 - 44	22,862,202	49.9	50.1	0.997	1.32*	1.08
	Age2: 45 - 54	23,309,611	56.1	43.9	1.278	1.69*	1.43*
	Age2: 55 - 64	14,913,382	57.4	42.6	1.347	1.78*	1.44*
	Age2: 65+	3,853,529	36.9	63.1	0.585	0.77*	0.68 *
Part/Full Time Status	Full-time	70,763,725	53.9	46.1	1.168	3.26*	1.62*
	Part-time	31,518,747	26.4	73.6	0.358		
Part/Full Year Status	Full-Year	97,047,824	47.0	53.0	0.885	4.46 *	2.47 *
	Part-Year	5,234,648	16.6	83.4	0.198		
Union Membership	1. Union	7,463,103	67.8	32.2	2.103	2.72*	2.00*
	2. Non-Union	94,819,369	43.6	56.4	0.774		
Gender	1. Male	54,394,487	47.2	52.8	0.895	1.17*	0.91*

Variable	Category	Total	Participating	Not Participating	Odds on Participating	Odds Ratio	Odds Ratio (Multivariate)
	2. Female	47,887,985	43.3	56.7	0.764		
Marital Status	1. Married	54,849,942	53.5	46.5	1.149	2.62*	1.19*
	2. Widowed	1,938,759	42.5	57.5	0.740	1.69*	0.97
	3. Divorced	11,429,738	50.4	49.6	1.017	2.32*	0.99
	4. Separated	2,174,048	36.8	63.2	0.582	1.33*	0.92
	5. Never Married	31,889,985	30.5	69.5	0.439		
Race/Ethnicity	1. White, Non-Hispanic	67,465,862	50.6	49.4	1.023		
	2. Black, Non-Hispanic	11,039,136	40.3	59.7	0.676	0.66 *	0.75 *
	3. Hispanic	16,358,256	27.2	72.8	0.374	0.37*	0.58 *
	4. Asian, Non-Hispanic	4,752,505	48.1	51.9	0.926	0.90	0.66 *
	5. Other, Non-Hispanic	2,666,713	42.6	57.4	0.743	0.73*	0.86
	Total	102,282,472	45.4	54.6	0.832		

Source: GAO analysis of weighted Survey of Income and Program Participation (SIPP) Data (2012). | GAO-15-556.

Note: Asterisks denote odds ratios which reflect differences that are statistically significant at the .05 level.

Table 10. Percentages of Workers of Different Types Whose Employers Do and Do Not Offer Retirement Programs, and Odds and Odds Ratios Derived from Them

Variable	Category	Total	Retirement Program Offered	No Retirement Program Offered	Odds On Program Offered	Odds Ratio	Odds Ratio (Multivariate)
Income Quartile	Lowest Quartile	25,569,365	40.3	59.7	0.675		
	2nd Quartile	25,493,645	55.7	44.3	1.259	1.87*	1.66*
	3rd Quartile	25,643,901	71.3	28.7	2.483	3.68*	2.71*
	Highest Quartile	25,575,562	83.9	16.1	5.219	7.73*	3.92*
Occupation	1. Management, Business, Science, and Arts Occupations	32,917,449	77.1	22.9	3.360	4.54 *	1.97*
	2. Service Occupations	18,465,079	42.5	57.5	0.739		
	3. Sales and Office Occupations	27,175,235	64.7	35.3	1.829	2.47*	1.61*
	4. Natural Resources, Construction, and Maintenance Occupations	9,619,204	48.6	51.4	0.945	1.28*	1.03
	5. Production, Transportation, and Material Moving Occupations	14,105,504	62.4	37.6	1.658	2.24*	1.50*

Variable	Category	Total	Retirement Program Offered	No Retirement Program Offered	Odds On Program Offered	Odds Ratio	Odds Ratio (Multivariate)
Education	1. LT HS Diploma	8,095,918	35.4	64.6	0.548	0.43*	0.73 *
	2. HS Diploma	26,703,135	55.8	44.2	1.262		
	3. Some College	37,213,439	63.5	36.5	1.738	1.38*	1.16*
	4. Bachelor's or More	30,269,980	75.6	24.4	3.090	2.45*	1.18*
Firm Size	1. More Than 1,000 Workers	44,333,968	81.6	18.4	4.431	9.22*	9.14*
	2. 501 to 1,000 Workers	4,822,085	75.6	24.4	3.094	6.44*	6.11*
	3. 101 to 500 Workers	13,086,877	72.6	27.4	2.648	5.51*	4.98 *
	4. 51 to 100 Workers	7,025,518	60.1	39.9	1.508	3.14*	2.95 *
	5. 50 or Fewer Workers	33,014,024	32.5	67.5	0.481		
Age	Age2: 18 - 24	13,224,335	45.4	54.6	0.831	0.49*	0.76 *
	Age2: 25 - 34	24,119,413	63.0	37.0	1.702		
	Age2: 35 - 44	22,862,202	63.9	36.1	1.767	1.04	0.88 *
	Age2: 45 - 54	23,309,611	68.7	31.3	2.194	1.29*	1.11
	Age2: 55 - 64	14,913,382	69.3	30.7	2.254	1.32*	1.05
	Age2: 65+	3,853,529	55.1	44.9	1.228	0.72*	0.62*
Part/Full Time Status	Full-time	70,763,725	68.2	31.8	2.146	2.09*	1.22*
	Part-time	31,518,747	50.7	49.3	1.029		
Part/Full Year Status	Full-Year	97,047,824	63.9	36.1	1.770	2.37*	1.54*
	Part-Year	5,234,648	42.8	57.2	0.747		

Table 10. (Continued)

Variable	Category	Total	Retirement Program Offered	No Retirement Program Offered	Odds On Program Offered	Odds Ratio	Odds Ratio (Multivariate)
Union Membership	1. Union	7,463,103	82.6	17.4	4.742	3.00*	2.01*
	2. Non-Union	94,819,369	61.3	38.7	1.582		
Gender	1. Male	54,394,487	63.4	36.6	1.733	1.06*	0.96
	2. Female	47,887,985	62.2	37.8	1.642		
Marital Status	1. Married	54,849,942	66.9	33.1	2.021	1.67*	1.11*
	2. Widowed	1,938,759	61.4	38.6	1.591	1.31*	1.09
	3. Divorced	11,429,738	66.6	33.4	1.991	1.64*	1.03
	4. Separated	2,174,048	59.1	40.9	1.445	1.19	1.18
	5. Never Married	31,889,985	54.8	45.2	1.213		
Race/Ethnicity	1. White, Non-Hispanic	67,465,862	67.4	32.6	2.068		
	2. Black, Non-Hispanic	11,039,136	62.9	37.1	1.695	0.82*	0.80 *
	3. Hispanic	16,358,256	44.5	55.5	0.802	0.39*	0.57 *
	4. Asian, Non-Hispanic	4,752,505	60.4	39.6	1.523	0.74*	0.55 *
	5. Other, Non-Hispanic	2,666,713	63.4	36.6	1.732	0.84	0.84
	Total	102,282,472	62.8	37.2	1.690		

Source: GAO analysis of weighted Survey of Income and Program Participation (SIPP) Data (2012). | GAO-15-556.

Note: Asterisks denote odds ratios which reflect differences that are statistically significant at the .05 level.

Table 11. Percentages of Workers of Different Types Who Are Eligible and Ineligible for the Retirement Programs Their Employers Offer, and Odds and Odds Ratios Derived from Them

Variable	Category	Total	Eligible	Not Eligible	Odds On Eligible	Odds Ratio	Odds Ratio (Multivariate)
Income Quartile	Lowest Quartile	10,304,214	56.0	44.0	1.272		
	2nd Quartile	14,208,542	82.8	17.2	4.810	3.78*	2.01*
	3rd Quartile	18,281,313	93.1	6.9	13.577	10.67*	4.35 *
	Highest Quartile	21,462,898	96.5	3.5	27.551	21.66*	7.52 *
Occupation	1. Management, Business, Science, and Arts Occupations	25,366,781	92.0	8.0	11.445	4.30*	1.21
	2. Service Occupations	7,848,882	72.7	27.3	2.660		
	3. Sales and Office Occupations	17,569,072	81.6	18.4	4.432	1.67*	0.94
	4. Natural Resources, Construction, and Maintenance Occupations	4,673,784	92.1	7.9	11.649	4.38*	1.28
	5. Production, Transportation, and Material Moving Occupations	8,798,449	86.4	13.6	6.334	2.38*	0.97
Education	1. LT HS Diploma	2,864,394	76.2	23.8	3.210	0.60*	0.80
	2. HS Diploma	14,900,315	84.2	15.8	5.316		
	3. Some College	23,622,812	83.9	16.1	5.197	0.98	0.80 *

Table 11. (Continued)

Variable	Category	Total	Eligible	Not Eligible	Odds On Eligible	Odds Ratio	Odds Ratio (Multivariate)
	4. Bachelor's or More	22,869,446	90.7	9.3	9.711	1.83*	0.70 *
Firm Size	1. More Than 1,000 Workers	36,171,148	85.8	14.2	6.027	1.00	1.27 *
	2. 501 to 1,000 Workers	3,644,348	86.1	13.9	6.194	1.03	1.18
	3. 101 to 500 Workers	9,499,033	86.9	13.1	6.661	1.11	1.14
	4. 51 to 100 Workers	4,224,392	86.7	13.3	6.511	1.08	1.09
	5. 50 or Fewer Workers	10,718,048	85.7	14.3	6.002		
Age	Age2: 18 - 24	6,000,057	48.9	51.1	0.956	0.17*	0.44 *
	Age2: 25 - 34	15,191,868	85.1	14.9	5.729		
	Age2: 35 - 44	14,598,763	91.4	8.6	10.573	1.85*	1.38 *
	Age2: 45 - 54	16,011,483	92.4	7.6	12.078	2.11*	1.56 *
	Age2: 55 - 64	10,330,876	92.3	7.7	12.016	2.10*	1.59 *
	Age2: 65+	2,123,920	82.0	18.0	4.562	0.80	0.73 *
Part/Full Time Status	Full-time	48,270,903	92.2	7.8	11.865	5.78*	2.56 *
	Part-time	15,986,065	67.3	32.7	2.054		
Part/Full Year Status	Full-Year	62,018,353	87.2	12.8	6.842	6.36*	3.12*
	Part-Year	2,238,615	51.8	48.2	1.076		
Union Membership	1. Union	6,163,455	91.5	8.5	10.752	1.83*	1.38 *
	2. Non-Union	58,093,513	85.4	14.6	5.865		
Gender	Male	34,491,780	88.4	11.6	7.624	1.53*	1.10
	Female	29,765,188	83.2	16.8	4.968		

Variable	Category	Total	Eligible	Not Eligible	Odds On Eligible	Odds Ratio	Odds Ratio (Multivariate)
Marital Status	Married	36,695,804	91.6	8.4	10.948	4.01*	1.43
	Widowed	1,190,516	83.5	16.5	5.070	1.86*	0.88
	Divorced	7,608,362	89.3	10.7	8.368	3.06	1.03
	Separated	1,284,829	82.5	17.5	4.700	1.72*	0.84
	Never Married	17,477,456	73.2	26.8	2.733		
Race/ Ethnicity	White, Non-Hispanic	45,473,443	86.9	13.1	6.633		
	Black, Non-Hispanic	6,942,898	82.3	17.7	4.647	0.70*	0.91
	Hispanic	7,281,447	83.0	17.0	4.877	0.74*	1.00
	Asian, Non-Hispanic	2,868,585	90.0	10.0	8.992	1.36*	0.96
	Other, Non-Hispanic	1,690,595	83.8	16.2	5.164	0.78	1.21
	Total	64,256,968	86.0	14.0	6.150		

Source: GAO analysis of weighted Survey of Income and Program Participation (SIPP) Data (2012). | GAO-15-556.

Note: Asterisks denote odds ratios which reflect differences that are statistically significant at the .05 level.

Table 12. Percentages of Workers of Different Types Participating and Not Participating in Retirement Programs, and Odds and Odds Ratios Derived from Them, for Workers Whose Employers Offer Retirement Programs for Which They Are Eligible

	Category	Total	Participating	Not Participating	Odds on Participating	Odds Ratio	Odds Ratio (Multivariate)
Income Quartile	Lowest Quartile	**5,768,713**	63.4	36.6	1.735		
	2nd Quartile	**11,763,009**	73.6	26.4	2.782	1.60*	1.22*
	3rd Quartile	**17,027,209**	86.2	13.8	6.242	3.60*	2.23 *
	Highest Quartile	**20,711,171**	93.9	6.1	15.440	8.90*	4.43 *
Occupation	1. Management, Business, Science, and Arts Occupations	**23,328,455**	90.2	9.8	9.252	4.05*	1.53 *
	2. Service Occupations	**5,704,097**	69.6	30.4	2.285		
	3. Sales and Office Occupations	**14,334,536**	81.9	18.1	4.512	1.97*	1.34 *
	4. Natural Resources, Construction, and Maintenance Occupations	**4,304,300**	84.6	15.4	5.506	2.41*	1.37 *
	5. Production, Transportation, and Material Moving Occupations	**7,598,715**	79.5	20.5	3.884	1.70*	1.17
Education	1. LT HS Diploma	**2,184,037**	67.2	32.8	2.048	0.54*	0.74 *
	2. HS Diploma	**12,541,175**	79.3	20.7	3.825		
	3. Some College	**19,810,619**	82.2	17.8	4.631	1.21*	0.97
	4. Bachelor's or More	**20,734,271**	90.4	9.6	9.390	2.46*	1.18

	Category	Total	Participating	Not Participating	Odds on Participating	Odds Ratio	Odds Ratio (Multivariate)
Firm Size	1. More Than 1,000 Workers	**31,023,957**	85.1	14.9	5.720	1.12	1.17
	2. 501 to 1,000 Workers	**3,137,735**	83.0	17.0	4.888	0.95	0.92
	3. 101 to 500 Workers	**8,259,137**	82.4	17.6	4.672	0.91	0.86
	4. 51 to 100 Workers	**3,661,940**	80.2	19.8	4.055	0.79	0.75 *
	5. 50 or Fewer Workers	**9,187,334**	83.7	16.3	5.127		
Age	Age2: 18 - 24	**2,932,209**	53.5	46.5	1.151	0.28*	0.46 *
	Age2: 25 - 34	**12,934,186**	80.4	19.6	4.094		
	Age2: 35 - 44	**13,337,350**	85.6	14.4	5.944	1.45*	1.26*
	Age2: 45 - 54	**14,787,150**	88.4	11.6	7.647	1.87*	1.67 *
	Age2: 55 - 64	**9,537,167**	89.8	10.2	8.760	2.14*	1.87 *
	Age2: 65+	**1,742,041**	81.7	18.3	4.459	1.09	0.90
Part/Full Time Status	Full-time	**44,518,662**	85.6	14.4	5.965	1.75*	1.14*
	Part-time	**10,751,441**	77.3	22.7	3.411		
Part/Full Year Status	Full-Year	**54,109,568**	84.2	15.8	5.339	1.81*	1.27
	Part-Year	**1,160,534**	74.7	25.3	2.951		
Union Membership	1. Union	**5,638,995**	89.7	10.3	8.702	1.73*	1.73 *
	2. Non-Union	**49,631,108**	83.4	16.6	5.017		
Gender	1. Male	**30,492,061**	84.3	15.7	5.360	1.04	0.84 *
	2. Female	**24,778,042**	83.7	16.3	5.140		
Marital Status	1. Married	**33,624,417**	87.2	12.8	6.830	2.16*	1.08
	2. Widowed	**994,393**	82.9	17.1	4.848	1.53*	0.86
	3. Divorced	**6,796,173**	84.8	15.2	5.584	1.76*	0.86
	4. Separated	**1,059,401**	75.5	24.5	3.081	0.97	0.73
	5. Never Married	**12,795,718**	76.0	24.0	3.164		

Table 12. (Continued)

	Category	Total	Participating	Not Participating	Odds on Participating	Odds Ratio	Odds Ratio (Multivariate)
Race/Ethnicity	1. White, Non-Hispanic	**39,516,204**	86.3	13.7	6.315		
	2. Black, Non-Hispanic	**5,713,495**	77.9	22.1	3.530	0.56*	0.74 *
	3. Hispanic	**6,042,577**	73.7	26.3	2.801	0.44*	0.67 *
	4. Asian, Non-Hispanic	**2,581,511**	88.5	11.5	7.690	1.22	0.97
	5. Other, Non-Hispanic	**1,416,317**	80.2	19.8	4.063	0.64*	0.91
	Total	**55,270,103**	**84.0**	**16.0**	**5.260**		

Source: GAO analysis of weighted Survey of Income and Program Participation (SIPP) Data (2012). | GAO-15-556.
Note: Asterisks denote odds ratios which reflect differences that are statistically significant at the .05 level.

Table 13. Summary Table of Unadjusted and Adjusted Odds Ratios Reflecting Differences in Participating, Comparing Self-Reported Data and "Corrected" Census Data (in Parentheses)

Variable	Category	(1) Unadjusted Odds Ratios (All Workers)	(2) Adjusted Odds Ratios (All Workers)	(3) Adjusted Odds Ratios (Eligible Workers)
Income	Lowest Quartile			
	2nd Quartile	3.08*	2.00*	1.22*
		(2.82)*	(1.94)*	(1.30)*
	3rd Quartile	8.01*	4.04*	2.23*
		(7.07)*	(3.79)*	(2.44)*
	Highest Quartile	19.01*	6.84*	4.43*
		(18.05)*	(6.84)*	(5.42)*

Variable	Category	(1) Unadjusted Odds Ratios (All Workers)	(2) Adjusted Odds Ratios (All Workers)	(3) Adjusted Odds Ratios (Eligible Workers)
Occupation	1. Management, Business, Science, and Arts Occupations	6.48*	1.95*	1.53
		(6.46)*	(1.95)*	(1.56)*
	2. Service Occupations			
	3. Sales and Office Occupations	2.78*	1.54*	1.34*
		(2.92)*	(1.71)	(1.45)*
	4. Natural Resources, Construction, and Maintenance Occupations	2.23*	1.25*	1.37*
		(1.98)*	(1.18)*	(1.47)*
	5. Production, Transportation, and Material Moving Occupations	2.74*	1.44*	1.17
		(2.68)*	(1.50)*	(1.22)
Education	1. LT HS Diploma	0.37*	0.61*	0.74*
		(0.40)*	(0.66)*	(0.68)*
	2. HS Diploma			
	3. Some College	1.31*	1.03*	0.97
		(1.39)*	(1.14)	(0.97)
	4. Bachelor's or More	2.74*	1.06*	1.18
		(2.95)*	(1.18)	(1.18)
Firm Size	1. More Than 1,000 Workers	4.85*	4.93*	1.17*
		(4.77)*	(4.89)*	(1.29)
	2. 501 to 1,000 Workers	3.87*	3.57*	0.92

Table 13. (Continued)

Variable	Category	(1) Unadjusted Odds Ratios (All Workers)	(2) Adjusted Odds Ratios (All Workers)	(3) Adjusted Odds Ratios (Eligible Workers)
		(4.03)*	(3.82)*	(1.05)
	3. 101 to 500 Workers	3.57*	3.01*	0.86
		(3.57)*	(3.10)*	(0.90)
	4. 51 to 100 Workers	2.37*	2.07*	0.75*
		(2.32)*	(2.07)*	(0.71)*
	5. 50 or Fewer Workers			
Age	Age2: 18 - 24	0.18*	0.37*	0.46*
		(0.24)*	(0.50)*	(0.43)*
	Age2: 25 - 34			
	Age2: 35 - 44	1.32*	1.08	1.26*
		(1.28)*	(1.06)	(1.20)*
	Age2: 45 - 54	1.69*	1.43*	1.67*
		(1.65)*	(1.41)*	(1.63)*
	Age2: 55 - 64	1.78*	1.44*	1.87*
		(1.68)*	(1.34)*	(1.75)*
	Age2: 65+	0.77*	0.68*	0.90
		(0.73)*	(0.63)*	(0.76)
Part/Full Time Status	Full-time	3.26*	1.62*	1.14*
		(3.34)*	(1.76)*	(1.14)
	Part-time			
Part/Full Year Status	Full-Year	4.46*	2.47*	1.27
		(3.69)*	(1.93)*	(1.28)
	Part-Year			

Variable	Category	(1) Unadjusted Odds Ratios (All Workers)	(2) Adjusted Odds Ratios (All Workers)	(3) Adjusted Odds Ratios (Eligible Workers)
Union Membership	1. Union	2.72*	2.00*	1.73*
		(2.55)*	(1.75)*	(1.60)*
	2. Non-Union	1.17*		
Gender Marital Status	1. Male		0.91*	0.84*
		(1.15)*	(0.92)*	(0.79)*
	2. Female			
	1. Married	2.62*	1.19*	1.08
		(2.48)*	(1.21)*	(1.11)
	2. Widowed	1.69*	0.97	0.86
		(1.59)*	(0.97)	(1.06)
	3. Divorced	2.32*	0.99	0.86
		(2.17)*	(0.96)	(0.85)
	4. Separated	1.33*	0.92	0.73
		(1.35)*	(1.01)	(0.78)
	5. Never Married			
Race/Ethnicity	1. White, Non-Hispanic			
	2. Black, Non-Hispanic	0.66*	0.75*	0.74*
		(0.72)*	(0.83)*	(0.75)*
	3. Hispanic	0.37*	0.58*	0.67*
		(0.37)*	(0.58)*	(0.71)*
	4. Asian, Non-Hispanic	0.90	0.66*	0.97
		(0.89)	(0.64)*	(0.91)
	5. Other, Non-Hispanic	0.73*	0.86	0.91
		(0.77)*	(0.91)	(0.85)

Source: GAO analysis of weighted Survey of Income and Program Participation (SIPP) Data (2012). | GAO-15-556.

Note: Asterisks denote odds ratios which reflect differences that are statistically significant at the .05 level.

End Notes

[1] In this report, "workplace retirement savings programs" include employee benefit plans, such as 401(k) plans, and employer provided Individual Retirement Accounts (IRAs), such as payroll deduction IRAs. The term does not include IRAs individuals may establish on their own outside the workplace.

[2] GAO, *Retirement Security: Most Households Approaching Retirement Have Low Savings*, GAO-15-419 (Washington, D.C., May 12, 2015). Outside of workplace retirement savings, other retirement savings include assets accrued through IRAs that individuals may establish on their own. Defined benefit plans are employee benefit plans that provide retirement benefits based on formulas that generally take into account an employee's salary and years of service.

[3] For more information on automatic enrollment, see GAO, *Retirement Savings: Automatic Enrollment Shows Promise for Some Workers, but Proposals to Broaden Retirement Savings for Other Workers Could Face Challenges*, GAO-10-31 (Washington, D.C.: Oct. 23, 2009). For prior research on trends in coverage, see: Craig Copeland, "Employment-Based Retirement Plan Participation: Geographic Differences and Trends, 2012," *Employee Benefit Research Institute*, Issue Brief No. 392, November 2013; and Alicia H. Munnell and Dina Bleckman, "Is Pension Coverage a Problem in the Private Sector?" *Center for Retirement Research at Boston College*, April 2014, No. 14-7.

[4] For more information on GAO's analysis of states' fiscal outlook, see: GAO, *State and Local Governments' Fiscal Outlook: 2014 Update*, GAO-15-224SP (Washington, D.C., Dec. 2014).

[5] To correct for self-reported error in the survey data, we compared a respondent's answer about participation in a workplace retirement savings program to information on their W-2 about contributions to a workplace retirement account. Specifically, the SIPP asks if the respondent's employer has any kind of pension or retirement plan for anyone in their company or organization. The W-2 includes contributions to the following workplace retirement savings programs: 401(k), 403(b), 408(k) and (p) (i.e., SEP and SIMPLE IRAs), 457, and 501 plans. If the respondent said "no, they do not participate," but they had positive contributions on their W-2 going to a workplace retirement savings program, we recoded them as a yes. Alternatively, if the respondent said "yes, they do participate" but there is no contribution evident in the W-2, we did not recode them as a no because we cannot rule out the possibility that their employer offers a defined benefit plan or defined contribution plan in which only the employer contributes.

[6] In this report, we use "state efforts" to refer to a range of activities that may have occurred in a state, including the introduction, action on or enactment of legislation, an executive action, or a study. We obtained information about recent state efforts from interviews with state government officials and knowledgeable industry representatives, as well as a review of legislative databases and other relevant websites. See appendix IV for the states we identified and a more detailed description of our methodology.

[7] Congress has established tax incentives to encourage employers to sponsor employee retirement plans, referred to in the Employee Retirement Income Security Act of 1974 (ERISA) as pension plans, and employees to participate in them. Employer contributions to qualified plans are a tax-deductible business expense, and, in general, contributions and investment earnings on those contributions are not taxed as income until the employee withdraws them from the plan.

[8] Congress authorized individual retirement accounts—popularly known as IRAs—which (1) provide a way for individuals not covered by a pension plan to save for retirement, and (2) give retiring workers or individuals changing jobs a way to preserve assets from employer-sponsored retirement plans by allowing them to roll over, or transfer, plan balances into IRAs.

[9] Investment Company Institute, The U.S. Retirement Market, Second Quarter 2012 (September 2012). http://www.ici.org/info/ret_12_q2_data.xls. See, GAO, *401(k) Plans: Labor and IRS Could Improve the Rollover Process for Participants*, GAO-13-30 (Washington, D.C., March 7, 2013). "Rollover" generally refers to a distribution from a 401(k) plan that an individual moves into another employee benefit plan or IRA, in order to avoid the funds being considered income and, thereby, immediately subject to income tax. Amounts taken from IRAs are generally referred to as "withdrawals," but may also be referred to as "distributions."

[10] See, for example, GAO-10-31, GAO, *Private Pensions: Alternative Approaches Could Address Retirement Risks Faced by Workers but Pose Trade-offs*, GAO-09-642 (Washington, D.C.: July 24, 2009), and GAO, *Private Pensions: Low Defined Contribution Plan Savings May Pose Challenges to Retirement Security, Especially for Many Low-Income Workers,* GAO-08-8 (Washington, D.C.: Nov. 29, 2007).

[11] Alicia H. Munnell and Dina Bleckman, "Is Pension Coverage a Problem in the Private Sector?" *Center for Retirement Research at Boston College*, April 2014, No. 14-7.

[12] Craig Copeland, "Employment-Based Retirement Plan Participation: Geographic Differences and Trends, 2012," Employee Benefit Research Institute, Issue Brief No. 392, November 2013.

[13] U.S. Department of Labor, Bureau of Labor Statistics, *Employee Benefits in the United States – March 2014*, USDL-14-1348.

[14] For example, the President has included the automatic IRA in each budget proposal since 2009.

[15] GAO-12-326.

[16] For more information on automatic enrollment, see GAO-10-31and GAO-09-642. For background on automatic enrollment and the automatic IRA, see: J. Mark Iwry and David C. John, *Pursuing Universal Retirement Security through Automatic IRAs*, testimony before the Subcommittee on Long-Term Growth and Debt Reduction, Committee on Finance, United States Senate, 109th Cong. June 29, 2006.

[17] 29 U.S.C. § 1104(c)(5). For a related GAO study on Qualified Default Investment Alternatives, see GAO, *401(k) Plans: Clearer Regulations Could Help Plan Sponsors Choose Investments for Participants, GAO-15-578 (Washington, D.C.: Aug. 25, 2015).*

[18] Pub. L. No. 109-280, §§ 621, 624 and 902, 120 Stat. 780, 978-79, 980, 1033-39 (codified as amended at 26 U.S.C. §§ 401(k)(13) and (m)(12), and 414(w), and 29 U.S.C. § 1104(c)), Default Investment Alternatives Under Participant Directed Individual Account Plans, 72 Fed. Reg. 60,452 (codified at 29 C.F.R. § 2550.404c-5) and Automatic Contributions Arrangements, 74 Fed. Reg. 8,200 (Feb. 24, 2009). Beginning in 1998, Treasury and Internal Revenue Service (IRS) rulings and other guidance first allowed employers to automatically enroll newly hired and current employees in 401(k), 403(b), and 457 retirement savings plans (Rev. Rul. 98-30, 1998-1 C.B. 1273. and Rev. Rul. 2000-8, 2000-2 C.B. 617; Rev. Rul. 2000-35, 2000-2 C.B. 138; Rev. Rul. 2000-33, 2000-1 C.B.142). A number of considerations inhibited more widespread adoption of automatic enrollment, including concerns such as liability in the event that the employee's investments under the plan did not perform satisfactorily, and concerns about state laws that prohibit withholding employee pay without written employee consent. PPA and subsequent regulations further

facilitated the adoption of automatic enrollment by providing incentives for doing so and by protecting plans from fiduciary and legal liability if certain conditions are met. In addition, in September 2009, Treasury announced IRS actions designed to further promote automatic enrollment and the use of automatic escalation policies. Rev. Rul. 2009-30, 2009-2 C.B. 391, and Notice 2009-65, 2009-2 C,B, 413. More recently, the IRS has further facilitated adoption of automatic enrollment and escalation features by providing for new correction procedures under its employee plans compliance resolution system. Rev. Proc. 2015-28, 2015-16 I.R.B. 920.

[19] Pub. L. No. 107-16, § 618, 115 Stat. 38, 106-08 (codified as amended at 26 U.S.C. § 25B). The Saver's Credit phases out at different earnings thresholds based on tax-filing status. For example, in 2015, the credit phases out completely for those who are married and filing a joint return if they earn more than $61,000. For more information on the Saver's Credit see GAO, *Automatic IRAs: Lower-Earning Households Could Realize Increases in Retirement Income*, GAO-13-699 (Washington, D.C.: Aug. 23, 2013) and GAO, *Private Pensions: Some Key Features Lead to An Uneven Distribution of Benefits*, GAO-11-333 (Washington, D.C.: March 30, 2011).

[20] Effective December 15, 2014, Treasury issued a final rule that made it possible for it to offer the retirement savings bond for *my*RA program. Regulations Governing Retirement Savings Bonds, 79 Fed. Reg. 74,023 (Dec. 15, 2014) (codified at 31 C.F.R. §§ 347.0- 347.52).

[21] The *my*RA investment will earn interest at the same variable rate as the Government Securities Investment Fund in the Thrift Savings Plan for federal employees. 31 C.F.R. § 347.40. Treasury officials noted that such a rate tends to keep up with inflation because it is tied to the weighted average of Treasury securities of a duration beyond 4 years—which already reflects expectations about and historically has kept pace with or exceeded inflation.

[22] 79 Fed. Reg. 74,023. *my*RA accounts follow Roth IRA rules. Accordingly, contributions are made with after-tax income and may be withdrawn tax-free at any time. In addition, earnings may be withdrawn at any time and may be withdrawn tax-free if the distribution is "qualified." A distribution is "qualified" if it is made at least 5 years after the owner's first contribution to the Roth IRA (counting from January 1 of the year of the first contribution), and the distribution is made for a qualifying reason, including after the owner is age 59 1/2. Because *my*RA accounts are Roth IRAs, their funds can actually be withdrawn and rolled into another Roth IRA at any time. 26 U.S.C. § 408A(d)(2)(A)(i) and (B).

[23] 26 U.S.C. § 408A(c)(3) and 26 C.F.R. § 1.408A-3. Annual income limits may change from year to year, but annual income limits in 2015 were $129,000 for individuals and $191,000 for couples.

[24] For more information on automatic IRAs see GAO-13-699 and GAO-10-31.

[25] Many of the state efforts we identified include features similar to the automatic IRA model. See appendix IV for a summary of the 29 state efforts we identified.

[26] For more information on multiple employer plans see GAO, *Private Sector Pensions: Federal Agencies Should Collect Data and Coordinate Oversight of Multiple Employer Plans*, GAO-12-665 (Washington, D.C.: Sept. 13, 2012).

[27] 29 U.S.C. § 1144. With certain exceptions, ERISA supersedes any and all state laws as they relate to any employee benefit plan covered under ERISA.

[28] Additionally, ERISA provides for the establishment of the Advisory Council on Employee Welfare and Pension Benefit Plans to advise and make recommendations to the Secretary of Labor with respect to carrying out the functions under ERISA. 29 U.S.C. § 1142.

[29] 29 U.S.C. §§ 1001b(a) and 1003(a), respectively.

[30] 26 U.S.C. § 4975 and 29 U.S.C. §§ 1106 and 1108(b).

[31] 29 U.S.C. § 1108(a).

[32] 26 U.S.C. §§ 401-461.

[33] 29 U.S.C. §§ 1052, 1053, and 1082, respectively.

[34] 26 U.S.C. §§ 410, 411 and 412, respectively.

[35] Employers may establish a retirement plan that "excludes" certain groups of employees in the sense that when voluntarily offering a retirement plan to some group or groups of employees, an employer may choose not to offer that plan or any retirement plan to another group or groups of employees.

[36] In addition, even when a plan would otherwise be available to them, employees may be ineligible to participate under a plan's provisions if they are under age 21 or have worked less than one year, which is defined as less than 1,000 hours in any 12-month period. 29 U.S.C. § 1052.

[37] 29 U.S.C. § 1144(a).

[38] 29 U.S.C. § 1144(b).

[39] 29 U.S.C. § 1144(c)(1).

[40] Shaw v. Delta Airlines, Inc., 463 U.S. 85, 96-97 (1983).

[41] Pilot Life Ins. Co. v. Dedeaux, 481 U.S. 41, 47-48 (1987).

[42] Metropolitan Life Ins. Co. v. Massachusetts, 471 U.S. 724, 740 (1985).

[43] The ERISA preemption provision covers "employee benefit plans," which includes employee welfare benefit plans, such as employer-sponsored health care benefits, as well as pension plans. 29 U.S.C. §§ 1002(3) and 1003(a).

[44] Golden Gate Rest. Ass'n v. City & County of San Francisco, 546 F.3d 639 (9th Cir. 2008), *cert. denied,* 561 U.S. 1024 (2010). A similar law in Maryland, however, was found by another federal appeals court to be preempted by ERISA. Retail Indus. Leaders Ass'n v. Fielder, 475 F.3d 180 (4th Cir. 2007).

[45] For purposes of this report, we use the term coverage to broadly refer to whether or not workers had access to a workplace retirement savings program (i.e., their employer offered a program for which the worker was eligible) and chose to participate. For specificity, we use distinct terms for participation, employer offer, and worker eligibility when reporting estimates from our data analysis. Figure 2 summarizes the use of these terms.

[46] The SIPP survey question generally asks about any retirement programs offered on the respondent's job. Specifically, it asks "Does your (job/business) have any kind of pension or retirement plans for anyone in your company or organization?" If the workers responds "yes" but indicates they are not included, a series of follow-up questions are asked about the reason(s) they are not included, some of which correspond to eligibility. See appendix I for a more detailed description.

[47] Irena Dushi, Howard Iams, and Jules Lichtenstein, "Assessment of Retirement Plan Coverage by Firm Size, Using W-2 Tax Records," *Social Security Bulletin*, Vol. 71, No. 2, 2011.

[48] If a respondent reported they did not participate in a plan, but actually had positive contributions to a workplace retirement program reported on their W-2, they were re-classified as participating. The data did not allow us to correct for the possibility that some participants may report they are participating when in fact they did not. This use of linked data is similar to the approach used in research by the Social Security Administration, which found that survey respondents tend to under-report participation. See Dushi, et. al. 2011.

[49] Further, as described in this report's following section, the effects of different factors on participation were very similar regardless of whether we used the self-reported data or the data corrected using the W-2 tax records.

[50] For example, we previously reported that many workers do not participate in retirement savings programs. However, from 1998 to 2009, working women's access to and participation in employer-sponsored retirement plans has improved relative to men. See: GAO, *Retirement Security: Women Still Face Challenges*, GAO-12-699 (Washington, D.C.: July 2012).

[51] Dushi, et. al., 2011.

[52] Irena Dushi, Howard Iams, and Jules Lichtenstein, "Retirement Plan Coverage by Firm Size: An Update," *Social Security Bulletin*, Vol.75 , No. 2, 2015.

[53] Bureau of Labor Statistics, "Employee Benefits in the United States – March 2014," USDL-14-1348, July 2014. In addition to the research described above, a study using 2012 CPS data found that 43 percent of all private sector workers ages 25 to 64 participated in a plan. See Alicia Munnell and Dina Bleckman, "Is Pension Coverage a Problem in the Private Sector?" Center for Retirement Research at Boston College, Issue Brief No. 14-7, April 2014. Using the same data for private sector workers ages 21 to 64, another study found that just over 39 percent participated in a plan. See Craig Copeland, "Employment-Based Retirement Plan Participation: Geographic Differences and Trends, 2012," *Employee Benefit Research Institute Issue Brief*, No. 392, November 2013.

[54] A worker may not be eligible, in effect, for a workplace retirement savings program offered by their employer based on several factors, including age, number of hours worked, location, or job category.

[55] For purposes of this study, we categorized respondents as being ineligible if they said they did not participate in a program their employer offers due to those in their type of job not being allowed in the program, not working enough hours, weeks, or months per year, their age, or not working long enough for this employer.

[56] We examined the likelihoods, or odds, of the following outcomes: 1) participating in a retirement program (among all private sector workers), 2) having an employer that offers a retirement program (among all private sector workers), 3) being eligible (among those offered programs), and 4) participating in a program (among those who are eligible). The regression models we used to estimate these likelihoods included variables for the following characteristics of workers: income, occupation, education, age, gender, marital status, race/ethnicity, size of the firm they worked for, whether they worked full-time or part-time, whether they worked for the full year or only part of the year, and whether they were or were not union members. For a detailed description of these results, see appendix VI.

[57] Odds ratios from the regression analysis using the public use SIPP data and W-2 adjusted data were similar in size and significance. As shown in figure 4, odds ratios comparing the likelihood of participation among those eligible for the second, third, and highest income quartiles compared to those in the lowest income quartile were 1.2, 2.2, and 4.4, respectively. Corresponding odds ratios from the W-2 adjusted data were 1.3, 2.4, and 5.4. Overall, the results of our regression analysis of participation using the self-reported measure in the public use data and the W-2 adjusted measure were very similar in the size and significance of variables included in our analysis.

[58] See GAO-12-326.

[59] The odds ratios from the regression analysis using self-reported participation and the W-2 adjusted data were similar—1.2 and 1.3, respectively—but the result was only statistically significant for the latter.

[60] Using the W-2 adjusted data, part-time status did not affect participation for workers who were eligible. While the odds ratio associated with full-time status was the same— odds ratio of

1.1—using self-reported participation or the W-2 adjusted data, the result was only statistically significant for the self-reported data.

61 Service sector workers were less likely to participate when they had access according to both the self-reported and W-2 adjusted data. Service sector occupations include cleaning, food preparation, hospitality, personal care and other services.

62 Under ERISA, plans may provide that workers otherwise eligible to participate in a plan are excluded from participating if they are younger than age 21 or have not been an employee for at least 1 year. GAO is currently conducting research on private sector employer-sponsored retirement plans' use of eligibility and vesting requirements and a report on that work is forthcoming. Results for the effect of age on participation were consistent between the self-reported and W-2 adjusted data. The odds ratios from the self-reported and W-2 adjusted data were 0.46 and 0.43, respectively.

63 Our discussion under this objective focuses on laws enacted or the most recent legislative efforts we identified in the six states we reviewed: California, Illinois, Maryland, Massachusetts, Washington and West Virginia. We selected these six states for case studies because they were identified as having "leading" state efforts by relevant government officials and knowledgeable industry representatives. As part of our review of these states, we analyzed state legislative materials and gathered testimonial evidence from knowledgeable industry representatives. While some of these states have enacted laws, none have fully implemented programs. Overall, we identified 29 states in which there has been some legislative effort to expand coverage in workplace retirement savings programs in recent years to mitigate future burdens on state social safety nets posed by retirement insecurity, including 11 states that have authorized studies to consider what, if anything, should be done to expand coverage. (See app. IV.) State officials and stakeholders noted that efforts to increase workers' access to workplace retirement savings programs will likely reduce the size of the currently uncovered population and help alleviate some pressure on social safety nets related to elder poverty. Furthermore, a stakeholder in one state noted that the state's economy is becoming increasingly dependent on retirees' income and spending. In these ways, state stakeholders saw legislative efforts that increase personal retirement savings as positive steps to building assets and protecting the state's fiscal condition. During the course of our work, we were also made aware that New York City has shown interest in expanding private sector coverage for New York City residents who lack access to a retirement program at work.

64 We reviewed 3 countries: Canada, New Zealand, and the United Kingdom. We did not conduct an independent legal analysis to verify the information provided about the laws, regulations, or policies of the countries selected for this study, but rather relied on secondary sources and interviews with knowledgeable officials in each country. In addition, the fact that a legal feature was successful in one or more of the countries we visited, which may have significantly different cultures, histories, and legal systems than the United States, does not necessarily indicate that it would be successful in the United States.

65 Automatic Enrolment in workplace pensions was introduced in the United Kingdom under the Pensions Act 2008 to address widespread under-saving for retirement.

66 Implementation started in 2012 with large employers in the United Kingdom and will continue into 2018 as the requirement starts to apply to small employers.

67 The United Kingdom's Department for Work and Pensions (DWP) initially anticipated an opt-out rate of approximately a third of all individuals automatically enrolled in the program. However, opt-out rates were between 9 and 10 percent in 2013, and approximately 12

percent in 2014. Given the success of automatic enrollment in the U.K., DWP has revised anticipated opt-out rates from 28 percent to 15 percent by 2018.

[68] As noted earlier, throughout this report we use "state efforts" to refer to a range of activities that may have occurred in a state, including the introduction of a bill, executive action, studies, or the enactment of legislation.

[69] ERISA defines a pension plan as established and maintained by an employer, employee organization, or both. 29 U.S.C. § 1002(2). At least one court has held that an entity that maintains a plan and the plan participants must have a common economic or representational interest, unrelated to the provision of benefits. *MDPhysicians & Associates, Inc. v. State Bd. Ins.*, 957 F.2d 178,185 (5th Cir. 1992), *cert. denied*, 506 U.S. 861 (1992).

[70] For example, the law in Illinois exempts employers with fewer than 25 employees and the law in California exempts employers with fewer than 5 employees.

[71] For example, a West Virginia official noted that the state has seen how offering access has been successful for public sector workers in the state's section 457 deferred compensation plan.

[72] Department of Labor's Employee Benefits Security Administration and Internal Revenue Service, *Choosing a Retirement Solution for Your Small Business*, (Washington, D.C., 2012); Accessed on June 22, 2015: http://www.dol.gov/ebsa/pdf/choosing.pdf; and Kobe, Kathryn. *Small Business Retirement Plan Availability and Worker Participation,* Written for the Small Business Administration, Office of Advocacy, (Washington, D.C., March 2010).

[73] While certain features of the programs we reviewed in states and other countries appear similar, we also recognize that there are important social, legal, and economic differences among these countries that could affect the success of their efforts.

[74] Canada would encourage employers in federally-regulated industries and most provinces to offer Pooled Registered Pension Plans (PRPP) through a licensed provider, while Quebec requires employers with five or more workers in the province that do not already offer a workplace retirement savings program to offer access to a licensed Voluntary Retirement Savings Plan (VRSP). Stakeholders noted that this effort would complement the existing industry, rather than crowd out plan providers, because it is designed to address the needs of middle income workers who are not saving enough to have adequate retirement income and are not currently offered a plan.

[75] The Washington law also includes life insurance plans that are designed for retirement purposes.

[76] See, for example: GAO-10-31; GAO-12-699; GAO-13-699; Jack VanDerhei and Craig Copeland, *The Impact of PPA on Retirement Savings for 401(k) Participants, 2008*, Issue Brief 318 (Washington D.C.: Employee Benefit Research Institute, June 2008); and Jeffrey W. Clark, Stephen P. Utkus, and Jean A. Young, *Automatic Enrollment: The Power of the Default.*(Vanguard Research, January 2015).

[77] GAO-10-31.

[78] Three years after employers automatically enrolled their workers they would be required to re-enroll those who opted out, except for any workers who opted out in the previous 12 months.

[79] Secure Choice programs in California and Illinois are structured as payroll deduction IRAs, which do not allow for employer contributions. Efforts in Maryland, Massachusetts, Washington, and West Virginia may allow employer contributions at the employer's discretion.

[80] Rather than deducting current contributions, Roth IRAs allow workers to make after-tax contributions and later withdraw their savings, including both principal and earnings, tax free.

[81] The kick-start contribution was available to new members of KiwiSaver until May 21, 2015. After this date, new members are no longer eligible for this payment.

[82] NEST has a public service obligation to accept any employer (and any qualifying worker) who wishes to use it.

[83] The U.K. government required that employers contribute, but decided to phase in contribution levels to reduce the burden for employers. Specifically, minimum employer contributions are being implemented in three phases from 2012 to 2018. Starting in October 2012, employers contributed 1 percent of qualifying earnings. Employer contribution levels will increase in October 2017 and finally in October 2018, when employers will need to remit required minimum contributions of 3 percent.

[84] NEST also has online tools such as communication templates and electronic member options for opt-outs to make it easier for employers. In 2012, NEST issued an updated pension "jargon buster" to help make pensions' terminology understandable for individuals.

[85] For example, qualified pension plans may require employees to attain the age of 21 or complete a year of service, whichever is later, before participating. 29 U.S.C. § 1052(a). A year of service means not less than 1,000 hours in a 12 month period. In addition, some stakeholders noted that certain unionized workers, such as some employed in the service sector, may not have a workplace retirement program and could also be excluded if their employer already offers a program to other workers.

[86] American Institute of Certified Public Accountants, "New AICPA Survey Reveals Effect, Regrets of Student Loan Debt," 2013, accessed May 25, 2015, http://www.aicpa.org/Press/PressReleases/2013/Pages/AICPA-Survey-Reveals-Effects-Regrets-Student-Loan-Debt.aspx. For more on the effect of student loan debt on the financial security of older Americans, see GAO, *Older Americans: Inability to Repay Student Loans May Affect Financial Security of a Small Percentage of Retirees,* GAO-14-866T (Washington, D.C.: Sept. 10, 2014).

[87] See GAO, *Retirement Income: Ensuring Income throughout Retirement Requires Difficult Choices*, GAO-11-400 (Washington, D.C.: June 7, 2011). In addition, people age 65 and older with low income and few assets may qualify for Supplemental Security Income (SSI), a means-tested program to provide cash assistance to people who are disabled, aged, or both. According to the Congressional Budget Office, the share of people age 65 and older who receive SSI is expected to fall from about 5 percent in 2011 to about 4 percent over the following 10 years. See: Congressional Budget Office, *Supplemental Security Income: An Overview*, December 2012.

[88] As indicated throughout this objective, the findings related to the potential legal challenges states could face given existing federal law and regulation arose chiefly out of discussions with state and national stakeholders about state efforts and our review of relevant documentation of those efforts. State efforts may or may not ultimately experience legal challenges and the outcomes of any challenges will depend on the facts and circumstances of how each program is implemented.

[89] At least one state not selected for review, Oregon, enacted legislation to increase coverage in workplace retirement savings programs. Oregon's governor signed the program into law on June 25, 2015. Among other things, employers would be required to automatically enroll their workers into the program established by the Oregon Retirement Savings Board unless

the employer offers a qualified retirement plan. See appendix IV for more information on Oregon's program.

[90] 29 U.S.C. § 1144(a).

[91] Stakeholders pointed to decisions by federal appeals courts that may provide some precedent for state questions regarding ERISA preemption. Retail Indus. Leaders Ass'n v. Fielder, 475 F.3d 180 (4th Cir. 2007) (striking down state law requiring certain employers to spend at least 8 percent of their total payroll on employees' health insurance) and Golden Gate Rest. Ass'n v. City & County of San Francisco, 546 F.3d 639 (9th Cir. 2008), *cert. denied,* 561 U.S. 1024 (2010) (upholding a similar state law).

[92] National stakeholders said that states that may be considering multiple employer plans would experience similar uncertainty. Multiple employer plans are a type of employee benefit plan covering employees of more than one employer. See GAO-12-665.

[93] The Massachusetts official told us that each participating employer would be considered to have created its own plan, characterizing the state's effort as development of a volume submitter 401(k) plan, which is a type of employee benefit plan that is typically pre-approved by the Internal Revenue Service.

[94] Payroll deduction IRAs are not considered employee benefit plans under ERISA so long as (1) there are no employer contributions, (2) employee participation is completely voluntary, (3) without endorsing the program, the employer limits its involvement to permitting the program to be publicized and providing for contributions to be made through payroll deduction, and (4) the employer receives only reasonable compensation for any services rendered in connection with the program. 29 C.F.R. § 2510.3-2(d). This, combined with Interpretive Bulletin 99-1, provided a roadmap in the form of a "safe harbor" to make it easier for employers to offer payroll deduction IRA arrangements that will not create employee benefit plans. Interpretive Bulletin 99-1; Payroll Deduction Programs for individual Retirement Accounts, 64 Fed. Reg. 33,000 (June 18, 1999) (codified at 29 C.F.R. § 2509.99-1). If an employer maintains neutrality with respect to an IRA sponsor in all its communications, it will not be viewed as endorsing the program. In addition, employers may reduce any administrative burden by selecting as few as one IRA sponsor to receive payroll contributions, and may be reimbursed by the IRA sponsor for the actual costs of operating the program.

[95] Some state laws, including those in California and Illinois, specify that the state cannot implement the program if it is determined to be an ERISA-covered employee benefit plan.

[96] On May 18, 2015, 26 Senators sent a letter to the President requesting that he ask DOL and Treasury to remove any potential uncertainty with respect to the application of federal law to state efforts by clarifying a number of issues and providing guidance.

[97] The Illinois law states: "The Board shall request in writing an opinion or ruling from the appropriate entity with jurisdiction over the federal Employee Retirement Income Security Act regarding the applicability of the federal Employee Retirement Income Security Act to the Program. The Board may not implement the Program if the IRA arrangements offered under the Program fail to qualify for the favorable federal income tax treatment ordinarily accorded to IRAs under the Internal Revenue Code or if it is determined that the Program is an employee benefit plan and State or employer liability is established under the federal Employee Retirement Income Security Act." 820 Ill.Comp. Stat. 80/95 (2015).

[98] Office of Management and Budget, *Fiscal Year 2016 Budget of the U.S. Government* (Washington, D.C., Feb. 2, 2015). Accessed on Feb. 12, 2015 at www.whitehouse.gov/omb/budget/overview. To better support state efforts, the President's Budget Submission would set aside $6.5 million at DOL, along with waiver authority, to

allow a limited number of states to implement state-based automatic enrollment IRAs or 401(k)-type programs.

[99] While DOL's Congressional Budget Justification specifies that funding would also allow management of grants by DOL's Chief Evaluation Office, which evaluates the performance and effectiveness of programs and activities, DOL officials told us that its oversight strategy still needs to be determined. Our previous work found gaps in payroll deduction IRA oversight and asked Congress to consider whether payroll deduction IRAs should have some direct DOL oversight. See GAO-08-590. DOL officials noted that they were unsure whether the pilot program would effectively grant DOL oversight authority over payroll deduction IRAs should those states that would use them be included in the program.

[100] 120 Stat 980, § 624(a) (codified at 29 U.S.C. § 1104(c)(5)).

[101] Final regulations issued by DOL specify four types of QDIAs. Default Investment Alternatives Under Participant Directed Individual Account Plans, 72 Fed. Reg. 60,452 (Oct. 24, 2007) (codified at 29 C.F.R. § 2550.404c-5(c)(4)). They are (1) a product with a mix of investments that takes into account an individual's age (such as a target-date fund), (2) an investment service that allocates assets according to an individual's age (such as a managed account), (3) a product with a mix of investments that takes into account the characteristics of the group of employees as a whole, rather than each individual (such as a balanced fund), or (4) a capital preservation fund that the sponsor may use as a QDIA for the first 120 days of an individual's participation to simplify administration if the worker opts out of the plan.

End Notes for Appendix I

[1] To provide context, we compiled a list of national legislative efforts proposed in recent years to expand coverage. We compiled this list through interviews with federal agency officials and knowledgeable industry representatives and targeted searches of legislative databases. See appendix III for additional information on our methodology and the selected list of federal legislative proposals.

[2] The survey contains catch-all questions for whether an individual's employer offers a DC plan, but it does not contain similar questions for DB plans. Specifically, those who are not included in their employer's plan are not asked whether their employer offers a DB plan.

[3] Irena Dushi, Howard Iams, and Julie Lichtenstein, "Assessment of Retirement Plan Coverage by Firm Size, Using W-2 Tax Records," *Social Security Bulletin*, Vol. 71, No. 2, 2011.

[4] We use "state efforts" to refer to a range of activities that may have occurred in a state, including the introduction of a bill, executive action, studies, or the enactment of legislation.

[5] Oregon Retirement Savings Task Force, *Report and Recommendations of the Oregon Retirement Savings Task Force: Created and Tasked Pursuant to HB 3436 (2013).* (Sept. 15, 2014).

[6] In addition, through a discussion with a knowledgeable international stakeholder we identified a specific program within the Australian superannuation system, the Small Business Superannuation Clearing House, which may help inform efforts to address administrative burdens for small employers in the United States. To learn more about this program, we completed a limited review of available documentation and interviewed a few targeted officials and stakeholders.

End Notes for Appendix II

[1] Governor's Task Force to Ensure Retirement Security for All Marylanders, *1,000,000 of Our Neighbors at Risk: Improving Retirement Security for Marylanders* (Annapolis, MD, February 2015).

[2] In a report prepared for AARP in August 2009, Optimal Benefit Strategies, LLC, summarized two industry surveys covering the use of manual payroll processing. Both surveys reported that less than 10 percent of employers did not use electronic payroll services. One survey reported that 9 percent of employers with 10 to 19 employees and fewer than 4 percent of employers with more than 20 employees do not use electronic payroll services. The other survey found that 3 percent of employers with between 10 and 49 employees do not use electronic payroll services. See Optimal Benefit Strategies, LLC. *Most Small Employers Face Low Costs to Implement Automatic IRAs.* (Aug. 19, 2009).

[3] For example, 2012 research found that two thirds of the 6.3 million private sector workers in California whose employer does not sponsor a retirement plan work for small employers with less than 100 employees. See Rhee, Nari. *6.3 Million Private Sector Workers in California Lack Access to a Retirement Plan on the Job*. Center for Labor Research and Education, University of California, Berkeley. (Berkeley, CA, June 2012).

[4] Illinois law also exempts employers that already offer a qualified plan or have been in business for less than 2 years. California law exempts employers that already offer a qualified plan or automatic enrollment payroll deduction IRA.

[5] For example, Massachusetts stakeholders noted that the level of take-up by employers of the state's voluntary program for not-for-profit employers with not more than 20 employees will likely be lower than if the program was required. For this and other reasons, they expected employer costs to be about the same as those for existing employee benefit plans for retirement—an annual amount larger than $2,000, which one not-for-profit stakeholder representative noted was higher than anticipated. They did feel that the advantages of the plan for participants would encourage employers to offer it. They expected investment management fees for participants to be lower and that the quality of the pooled, professionally managed investments would entice employers to offer this plan.

[6] The government considered excluding some very small employers from the automatic enrollment requirements, but ultimately decided against exclusion in order to ensure broader workplace access to retirement plans. The phase-in began in October 2012, when employers with 120,000 or more employees became subject to the automatic enrollment requirements. The final phase of implementation will begin when the smallest employers (fewer than 50 employees) will be required to automatically enroll employees (between June 2015 and April 2017).

[7] The Pensions Commission also noted that a large number of accounts of individuals are unprofitable, particularly those of lower earners. As a result, a NEST representative said the target market for NEST was always anticipated to be lower income workers and those who are more likely to switch jobs because these types of accounts have a lower economic value for commercial providers. While this representative thought that a good chunk of larger employers would have employees that fit this description, NEST anticipated that the vast majority of employers it would eventually serve would be very small. Because these employers had not yet been phased in to the employer requirement, as of December 2014 the NEST representative estimated NEST had enrolled less than 2 percent of the total number of employers it will eventually bring on.

[8] We have previously reported on the burdens small employers face in starting and administering plans. See GAO, *Private Pensions: Better Agency Coordination Could Help Small Employers Address Challenges to Plan Sponsorship*, GAO-12-326 (Washington, D.C., March 5, 2012).

[9] While programs seek to minimize employer duties, participating employers will need to take some action. To avoid confusion, stakeholders noted that states plan to educate employers about the details of the program and their responsibilities for worker outreach. For example, the Massachusetts Treasurer's office is working on a checklist to educate employers about their responsibilities with respect to the program which will include nondiscrimination testing and timely remittance of contributions, among other things.

[10] According to stakeholders in Washington State, the implementation phase for the marketplace effort is expected to begin in July 2015 with the goal of full implementation by 2017.

[11] Stakeholders in Illinois, Maryland, and West Virginia expected to be able to borrow money from the state to fund startup costs, which would be paid back through participant fees once the programs are implemented. Stakeholders in Washington estimated that designing and implementing the marketplace would cost about $200,000, but expected to incur additional costs to conduct marketing and outreach since the program is voluntary for employers and workers. They discussed the possibility of providing financial incentives to employers to participate. Stakeholders in Illinois and Washington said they may also secure private funds from foundations to help pay for implementation costs.

End Notes for Appendix III

[1] We attempted to identify legislative proposals and executive actions between 2009 and July 28, 2015, but multiple states may have proposed legislation prior to 2009. We have included select efforts that occurred before 2009 if they were noted by knowledgeable industry stakeholders or if we determined through our research that the state had not already been captured in the table.

[2] We used the following search terms to identify state efforts on LexisNexis and WestLaw: 1) state private worker pension plan policies, 2) state private worker pension plans, 3) state private sector worker retirement savings plan policies, 4) state private sector worker retirement savings policies, 5) state automatic individual retirement accounts, 6) state IRAs, 7) state secure choice plans, 8) state-run private retirement plans, 9) state-run private retirement savings, and 10) state private pension savings.

End Notes for Appendix VI

[1] This value, and the other values of the odds shown in the tables, may not equal precisely what one obtains by dividing the percentages shown in the table, since the tabled values were estimated directly from the numbers on which the percentages were based to avoid rounding error.

[2] The only difference (or ratio) shown in the table which is not statistically significant involves the difference between Asians and Whites, where the odds ratio is 0.9, or very nearly 1.0, which indicates no difference in the odds on participating.

In: Retirement Security
Editor: Rafael Wilkins

ISBN: 978-1-63485-000-1

Chapter 2

PRIVATE PENSIONS: LOW DEFINED CONTRIBUTION PLAN SAVINGS MAY POSE CHALLENGES TO RETIREMENT SECURITY, ESPECIALLY FOR MANY LOW-INCOME WORKERS*

United States Government Accountability Office

WHY GAO DID THIS STUDY

Over the last 25 years, pension coverage has shifted primarily from "traditional" defined benefit (DB) plans, in which workers accrue benefits based on years of service and earnings, toward defined contribution (DC) plans, in which participants accumulate retirement balances in individual accounts. DC plans provide greater portability of benefits, but shift the responsibility of saving for retirement from employers to employees. This report addresses the following issues: (1) What percentage of workers participate in DC plans, and how much have they saved in them? (2) How much are workers likely to have saved in DC plans over their careers and to what degree do key individual decisions and plan features affect plan saving? (3) What options have been recently proposed to increase DC plan coverage,

* This is an edited, reformatted and augmented version of a United States Government Accountability Office publication, No. GAO-08-8, dated November 2007.

participation, and savings? GAO analyzed data from the Federal Reserve Board's 2004 Survey of Consumer Finances (SCF), the latest available, utilized a computer simulation model to project DC plan balances at retirement, reviewed academic studies, and interviewed experts.

What GAO Recommends

GAO is not making any recommendations.

What GAO Found

GAO's analysis of 2004 SCF data found that only 36 percent of workers participated in a current DC plan. For all workers with a current or former DC plan, including rolled-over retirement funds, the total median account balance was $22,800. Among workers aged 55 to 64, the median account balance were $50,000, and those aged 60 to 64 had $60,600 (see figure below). Low-income workers had less opportunity to participate in DC plans than the average worker, and when offered an opportunity to participate in a plan, they were less likely to do so. Modest balances might be expected, given the relatively recent prominence of 401(k) plans.

Projections of DC plan savings over a career for workers born in 1990 indicate that DC plans could on average replace about 22 percent of annualized career earnings at retirement for all workers, but projected "replacement rates" vary widely across income groups and with changes in assumptions. Projections show almost 37 percent of workers reaching retirement with zero plan savings. Projections also show that workers in the lowest income quartile have projected replacement rates of 10.3 percent on average, with 63 percent of these workers having no plan savings at retirement, while highest-income workers have average replacement rates of 34 percent. Assuming that workers offered a plan always participate raises projected overall savings and reduces the number of workers with zero savings substantially, particularly among lower-income workers.

Recent regulatory and legislative changes and proposals could have positive effects on DC plan coverage, participation, and savings, some by facilitating the adoption of automatic enrollment and escalation features. Some options focus on encouraging plan sponsorship, while others would create accounts for people not covered by an employer plan. Our findings indicate that DC plans can provide a meaningful contribution to retirement security for some workers but may not ensure the retirement security of lower-income workers.

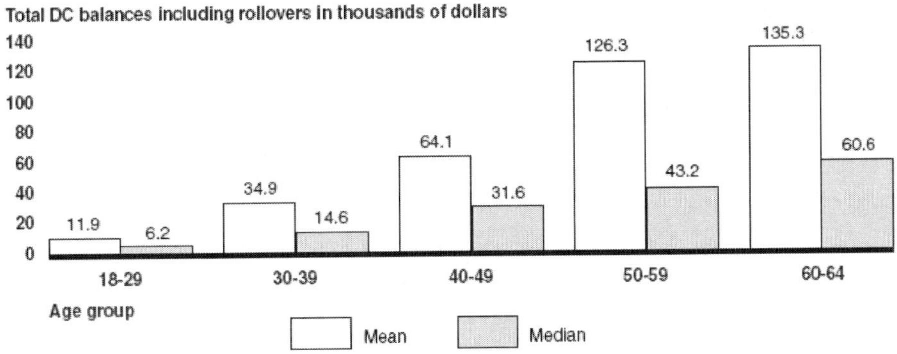

Source: GAO analysis of 2004 Survey of Consumer Finances.

Total DC Balances for Workers with a Current or Former DC Plan, Including Rolled-Over Retirement Funds, by Age Group, 2004 SCF.

ABBREVIATIONS

AWI	average wage index
BLS	Bureau of Labor Statistics
CODA	cash or deferred arrangement
CPS	Current Population Survey
CRS	Congressional Research Service
DB	defined benefit
DC	defined contribution
EBRI	Employee Benefit Research Institute
EBSA	Employee Benefits Security Administration
ERISA	Employee Retirement and Income Security Act of 1974
ESOP	employee stock ownership plan
HRS	Health and Retirement Study
ICI	Investment Company Institute
IRA	individual retirement account
MINT3	Modeling Income in the Near Term

OCACT	Office of the Chief Actuary
PPA	Pension Protection Act of 2006
PSG	Policy Simulation Group
PSID	Panel Study of Income Dynamics
SCF	Survey of Consumer Finances
SEP	Simplified Employee Pension Plan
SIMPLE	Savings Incentive Match Plan for Employees of Small Employers
SIPP	Survey of Income and Program Participation
SSA	Social Security Administration
UA	universal account

* * *

November 29, 2007

The Honorable George Miller
Chairman
Committee on Education and Labor
House of Representatives

Dear Mr. Chairman:

Employer-sponsored pensions represent an important component of retirement income. Since the early 1980s, while the percentage of workers participating in a pension plan has remained around 50 percent of the private sector work force, pension coverage has seen a noticeable shift away from "traditional" defined benefit (DB) plans, in which workers typically accrue benefits based on years of service and earnings, toward defined contribution (DC) plans, in which participants accumulate balances in personal accounts. DC plans provide participants tax-preferred savings vehicles, portability, and the transparency of known account balances. However, they shift the responsibility of saving for retirement, and certain key risks, from employers to employees. Under such plans, workers often manage the investment of plan assets throughout their lives. However, workers may receive limited or no contributions from their employers, spend accumulated savings prior to retirement, or choose not to participate in a pension plan at all, ultimately arriving at retirement with insufficient savings to support themselves. Further, retirees usually must manage their DC plan savings to make them last throughout retirement. Possible reforms to Social Security to address that program's long-term solvency could reduce benefits for future retirees, possibly increasing the future role of DC plans, as well as other personal savings, in providing retirement income.[1]

Based on these concerns, this report addresses the following questions: (1) What percentage of workers participate in DC plans, and how much have they saved in them? (2) How much are workers likely to have saved in DC plans by the time they reach retirement and to what degree do certain key individual decisions and plan features affect plan saving? (3) What options have been recently proposed to increase DC plan coverage, participation, and savings?

To analyze participation and savings in DC plans, we examined data from the 2004 version of the Federal Reserve Board's Survey of Consumer Finances (SCF), the latest available SCF, and data published by other government agencies, by private organizations, and from academic studies. [2] To analyze how much Americans can expect to save in DC plans by the time they retire and the factors that affect these savings, we utilized a microsimulation model, PENSIM, that simulates demographic, working, and pension patterns for a constructed sample over their lives. (See appendix I for further details of our projections using PENSIM.) We also reviewed similar studies to compare their methodologies and conclusions (see app. II). To analyze policy options to increase DC plan coverage, participation, and savings, we synthesized information gathered from interviews of plan practitioners, financial managers, and public policy experts, as well as from academic and policy studies on DC plan participation and savings. We also researched current government initiatives and policy proposals to broaden participation in account-based pension plans and increase retirement savings. We conducted our work from July 2006 to October 2007 in accordance with generally accepted government auditing standards.

RESULTS IN BRIEF

Regardless of the age of the individual, and at most income levels, DC account participation is low, and the account balances of workers participating in DC plans are modest. According to our analysis of the 2004 SCF, shows that only 36 percent of workers were participating in a DC plan with their current employer. For all workers with a current or former DC plan, including funds rolled over into a new plan or an IRA, the median account balances measured $22,800. Among workers aged 55 to 64 with a current or former DC plan, including rolled over retirement funds, the median account balance was $50,000, which if converted into an annuity at age 65 would represent about $4,400 per year for life. While we might expect older workers to have limited balances in DC plans because relatively few employers started offering such plans until the 1980s, thus not giving older workers the opportunity to save in them for their whole careers, it is notable that DC plan savings will be only a limited component of retirement income for this group. Leakage, or the cashing out of lump-sum distributions for non-retirement purposes, could adversely affect account accumulation for some plan participants. From our analysis of the 2004 SCF, of the 21 percent of households reporting that they had previously received lump-sum distributions from previous jobs' retirement plans, about 47 percent cashed out all the funds, 4 percent cashed out some of the funds, and 50 percent rolled over all the funds into another retirement account. Low-income workers had the opportunity to participate in DC plans less frequently than the average worker, and when they were offered a plan, they were less likely to do so. As a result, only 8 percent of workers in the lowest income quartile participated in DC plans with their current employer.

Simulations of future workers' DC plan savings over an entire working career indicate that DC plans could replace, on average, about 22 percent of annualized career earnings at retirement, but with projected replacement rates varying widely across income groups and with changes in certain assumptions. These projections show that individuals in this cohort would accumulate enough DC plan savings over their careers to produce average annuitized retirement income of $18,784 (in 2007 dollars) per year, but also that about 37 percent of the sample population would have zero savings from DC plans when they retire. Workers in the lowest income quartile have projected replacement rates of 10.3 percent on average, but 63 percent of these workers are projected to have no DC savings at retirement. Highest-income workers, in contrast, have average projected replacement rates of almost 34 percent from DC plans. Workers who are eligible to participate in a plan for at least 15 years have an average projected replacement rate of 33.5 percent, but about 16 percent of these workers still have no projected savings at retirement. Some changes in assumptions in our projections indicate that certain key individual behaviors or plan features have a significant impact on plan savings, especially for low-income workers, and on the number of workers with zero savings at retirement. Assuming that all workers who are offered a plan always participate in it would raise average retirement income from DC plans by about 40 percent, with particularly high increases to lowest-income workers and a reduction in the number of workers who do not save at all. Assuming that workers do not withdraw money from their accounts while they are working—that is, no leakage occurs—raises overall average annuity income from DC plans by about 11 percent and reduces the percentage of those with no DC savings at retirement by over 25 percent. Other scenarios, such as working longer or raising contribution limits, raised savings primarily for higher-income workers, and reduced the number of workers with zero savings at retirement only slightly.

Recent regulatory and legislative changes and proposals could have positive effects on DC plan coverage, participation, and savings. Some of these have facilitated plan sponsors' adoption of automatic enrollment and automatic escalation of contributions, which some studies indicate may increase DC participation and savings among workers who already have access to a plan. Other proposals focus on encouraging more employers to sponsor plans in order to increase plan participation and savings. In one, the "State-K" proposal, states would collaborate with private financial institutions to offer employers the option of adopting a state-designed low-cost plan. Broader options, such as the automatic individual retirement account (IRA) or universal accounts proposals, would seek to extend retirement account coverage by facilitating savings in IRAs or creating retirement savings vehicles for people not covered by a voluntary employer based retirement plan. Another would expand the saver's credit by making it refundable to workers who pay little or no federal income tax. It is important to note that Social Security benefits provide the bulk of retirement benefits for most households; evaluations of income security should consider total retirement income from all sources, not just DC plans.

BACKGROUND

Employer-sponsored pensions fall into two major categories: defined benefit (DB) and defined contribution (DC) plans. In DB, or traditional, plans, benefits are typically set by formula, with workers receiving benefits upon retirement based on the number of years worked for a firm and earnings in years prior to retirement.[3] In DC plans, workers accumulate savings through contributions to an individual account. These accounts are tax-advantaged in that contributions are typically excluded from current income, and earnings on balances grow tax-deferred until they are withdrawn.[4] An employer may also make contributions, either by matching employee's contributions up to plan or legal limits, or on a non-contingent basis.

Like DB plans, DC plans operate in a voluntary system with tax incentives for employers to offer a plan and for employees to participate. Contributions to and earnings on DC plan accounts are not taxed until the participant withdraws the money, although participants making withdrawals prior to age 59 1/2 may incur an additional 10 percent tax.[5] In 2006, the pension tax expenditure for DC plans amounted to $54 billion.[6] In addition, a nonrefundable tax credit to qualifying low-and middle-income workers who make contributions, the saver's credit, accounted for less than 2 percent of the 2006 tax expenditure on account-based retirement plans.[7]

DC plans offer workers more control over their retirement asset management, but also shift some of the responsibility and certain risks onto workers. Workers generally must elect to participate in a plan and make regular contributions into their plans over their careers. Participants typically choose how to invest plan assets from a range of options provided under their plan, and accordingly face investment risk.[8] Savings in DC plans are portable in the sense that a participant may keep plan balances in a tax-protected account upon leaving a job, either by rolling over plan balances into a new plan or an IRA, or in some cases leaving money in an old plan.[9] Workers may have access to plan savings prior to retirement, either through loans or withdrawals; participants may find such features desirable, but pre-retirement access may also lead to lower retirement savings (sometimes referred to as leakage) and possible tax penalties. Workers who receive DC distributions in lump-sum form must manage account withdrawals such that their savings last throughout retirement. In contrast, a formula, often based on preretirement average pay and years of service, determines DB plan benefits, and workers are usually automatically enrolled in a plan. The employer has the responsibility to ensure that the plan has sufficient funding to pay promised benefits, although the sponsor can choose to terminate the plan.[10] DB plans also typically offer the option to take benefits as a lifetime annuity, or periodic benefits until death. An annuity provides longevity insurance against outliving one's savings, but may lose purchasing power if benefits do not rise with inflation. Table 1 summarizes some of the primary differences between DC and DB plans.

Table 1. Key Characteristics of Defined Contribution and Defined Benefit Plans

	Defined contribution plans	Defined benefit plans
What determines the level of benefits?	Contributions into a personal account and the return on assets.	A formula, typically based on years of service and salary history.
What does the employee have to do to participate and earn benefits in the plan?	May require waiting for eligibility and sign-up by employee. Participants may need to work up to 6 years to fully vest in employer matching contributions	Eligibility and participation are typically automatic. Workers working at least 1,000 hours per year earn years of service toward benefits. Participants may need to work for up to 7 years to fully vest in plan benefits.
How are contributions made?	Typically, employee decides how much to contribute from current wages; employer may also contribute.	Typically by employer only, except in some public sector plans.
Who manages the assets and assumes the risks of investing it?	Employee, in most plans.	Plan sponsor; benefits are government-insured up to certain limits.
What happens to the benefits when the employee leaves the job?	Can be left in plan, rolled over to an IRA, or cashed out (often with a penalty if done before age 59 ½)	Sometimes unavailable until beneficiary reaches specified retirement age.
How are benefits taken in retirement and what are the major risks they pose?	Typically by withdrawing from total balances, and must be managed to last throughout retirement.	Typically payable as life annuities, but plan may offer lump sum option. Annuities lose purchasing power over time if not indexed to inflation.

Source: GAO analysis.

Over the past 25 years, DC plans have become the dominant type of private sector employee pension. In 1980, private DB plans had 38 million participants, while DC plans had 20 million. As of 2004, 64.6 million participants had DC plans, while 41.7 million had DB plans. Further, over 80 percent of private sector DC participants in 2004 were active participants (in a plan with their current employer), while about half of DB participants had separated from their sponsoring employer or retired. According to the Employee Benefit Research Institute (EBRI), while overall pension coverage among families remained around 40 percent between 1992 and 2001, 38 percent of families with a pension relied exclusively on a DC plan for retirement coverage in 1992, while 62 percent had a DB plan. In 2001, 58 percent of pension-participating families had only a DC plan, while 42 percent had a DB plan.[11] Assets in all DB plans exceeded total DC assets as recently as 1995. As of 2006, DC plans had almost $3.3 trillion in assets while DB plans had almost $2.3 trillion. In addition, assets in IRAs, accounts that are also tax protected and include assets from rolled-over balances from employer-sponsored plans, measured over $4.2 trillion in 2006.

There are several different categories of DC plans. Most of these plans are types of cash or deferred arrangements (CODA), in which employees can direct pre-tax dollars, along with any employer contributions, into an account, with assets growing tax deferred until withdrawal. The 401(k) plan is the most common, covering over 85 percent of active DC participants. Certain types of tax-exempt employers may offer plans, such as 403(b) or 457 plans, which have many features similar to 401(k) plans. Many employers match employee contributions, generally based on a specified percentage of the employee's salary and the rate at which the participant contributes.[12] Small business owners may offer employees a Savings Incentive Match Plan for Employees of Small Employers (SIMPLE) or a Simplified Employee Pension Plan (SEP), two types of DC plans that have reduced regulatory requirements for sponsors. Other types of DC plans keep the basic individual account structure of the 401(k), but with different requirements and employer practices. Some are designed primarily for employer contributions. These include money purchase plans, which specify fixed annual employer contributions; profit sharing plans, in which the employer decides annual contributions, perhaps based on profits, into the plan, and allocations of these to each participant; and employee stock ownership plans (ESOPs), in which contributions are primarily invested in company stock.[13]

Building up retirement savings in DC plans rests on factors that are, to some degree, outside of the control of the individual worker, as well as behaviors an individual does control (see fig. 1). Factors outside the individual's direct control include the following:

- **Plan sponsorship**—the employer's decision to sponsor a plan, as well as participation eligibility rules.
- **Employer contributions**—whether the sponsor makes matching or noncontingent contributions.
- **Investment options**—the plan sponsor's decisions about investment options to offer to participants under the plan.
- **Market returns on plan assets**—market performance of plan assets.

Key individual decisions and behaviors that may affect retirement savings include the following:

- **Employee contributions**—deposits into the plan account, typically out of current wages.
- **Investment decisions**—how to invest plan assets given investment options offered under the plan.
- **Withdrawals/loans**—pre-retirement withdrawals from account balances, which usually incur a tax penalty. Similarly, taking out a loan from a plan, if allowed, may reduce future balances if the loan is not repaid in full and treated as a withdrawal, or by lowering investment returns.
- **Rollover**—upon separation from a job, a participant may transfer the plan account balance to an IRA, which maintains most of the same tax preferences on the balances, move it to a new tax-qualified plan, or leave the money in the old plan. Alternatively, any cash withdrawal would likely be subject to income tax and penalties.
- **Age at retirement**—the decision as to when to retire determines how many years the worker has to accumulate plan balances and how long the money has to last in retirement.

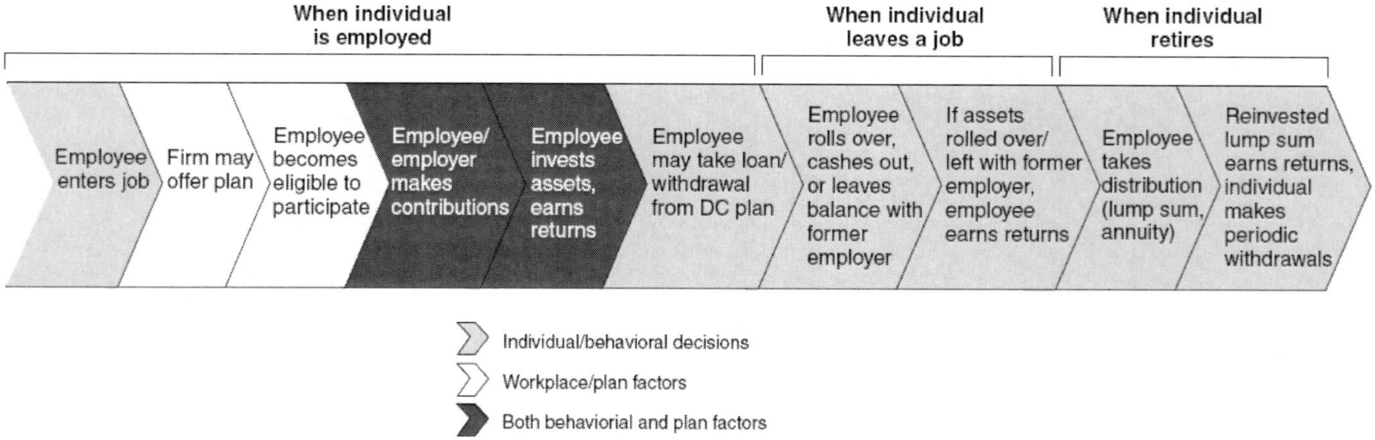

Source: GAO analysis.

Figure 1. Mechanics of Accumulating Retirement Savings in DC Plans.

There is little consensus about how much constitutes "enough" savings to have going into retirement. We may define retirement income adequacy relative to a standard of minimum needs, such as the poverty rate, or to the consumption spending that households experienced during working years.[14] Some economists and financial advisors consider retirement income adequate if the ratio of retirement income to pre-retirement income—or replacement rate—is between 65 and 85 percent. Retirees may not need 100 percent of pre-retirement income to maintain living standards for several reasons. Retirees will no longer need to save for retirement, retirees' payroll and income tax liability will likely fall, work expenses will no longer be required, and mortgages and children's education and other costs may have been paid off.[15] However, some researchers cite uncertainties about future health care costs and future Social Security benefit levels as reasons to suggest that a higher replacement rate, perhaps above 100 percent or higher, would be considered adequate.[16]

To achieve adequate replacement rate levels, retirees depend on different sources of income to support themselves in retirement. Social Security benefits provide the bulk of retirement benefits for most households. As of 2004, annuitized pension benefits provided almost 20 percent of total income to households with someone age 65 or older, while Social Security benefits provided 39 percent.[17] Social Security benefits compose over 50 percent of total income for two-thirds of households with someone age 65 or older, and at least 90 percent of income for one-third of such households. Table 2 shows estimated replacement rates from Social Security benefits for low and high earners retiring in 2007 and 2055, as well as the remaining amount of pre-retirement income necessary to achieve a 75 percent replacement rate.[18] These figures give rough guidelines for how much retirement income workers might need from other sources, such as employer-sponsored pensions, as well as earnings and income from other savings or assets.

It is important to keep certain economic principles in mind when evaluating the effectiveness of retirement accounts, or any pensions, in providing retirement income security. First, balances accumulated in a DC plan may not represent new saving; individuals may have saved in another type of account in the absence of a DC plan or its tax preferences. Second, evaluating worker income security should consider total compensation, not just employer contributions to DC plans. All else equal, we should generally expect more generous employer-sponsored pension benefits to lower cash wages and that the split between current wages and deferred compensation is largely a reflection of labor market conditions, tax provisions, and worker and employer preferences.

Table 2. Estimated Social Security Replacement Rates for Workers Turning 65 in 2007 and in 2055, Percent of Career-Average Earnings

	Year in which a 65 year old retires			
	2007		2055	
Source of replacement rate income	Low earner	High earner	Low earner	High earner
Social Security	54.2	33.5	49.0	30.1
Replacement from other sources to achieve 75 percent replacement rate	20.8	41.5	26.0	44.9

Source: The 2007 Annual Report of the Board of Trustees of the Federal Old-Age and Survivors Insurance and Federal Disability Insurance Trust Funds, Table VI.F10.

Note: Based on scheduled benefits under intermediate assumptions of Social Security projections. Replacement rates represent benefits as a percentage of career-average earnings for low and high earners.

Many Workers Have No Plan Coverage, and Most DC Plan Participants Currently Have Modest Account Balances

Many workers do not have DC plans, and median savings levels among participants show modest balances. While it is worth noting that for workers nearing retirement age, DC plans were not considered primary pension plans for a significant portion of their working careers, participation rates and median balances in such plans are low across all ages. Only 36 percent of working individuals were actively participating in a DC plan, according to data from the 2004 SCF.[19] Further, workers aged 55 to 64 had median balances totaling $50,000 in account-based retirement savings vehicles, including DC plans and rollover accounts.[20] Leakage, when workers withdraw DC savings before retirement age, can also reduce balances; almost half of those taking lump-sum distributions upon leaving a job reported cashing out their balances for non-retirement purposes. Participation among lower-income workers was particularly limited, and those who did have accounts had very low balances.

Most Workers Do Not Have a Current DC Plan, and Participants Have Modest Plan Balances

The majority of workers, in all age groups, are not participating in DC plans with their current employers. Employers do not always offer retirement plans, and when they do, plans may have eligibility restrictions initially, and some eligible workers do not choose to participate.[21] According to our analysis of the 2004 SCF, only 62 percent of workers were offered a retirement plan by their employer, and 84 percent of those offered a retirement plan participated.[22] Only 36 percent of working individuals participated in a DC plan with their current employer (see fig. 2). Data indicated similar participation rates for working households, as 42 percent of households had at least one member with a current DC plan.

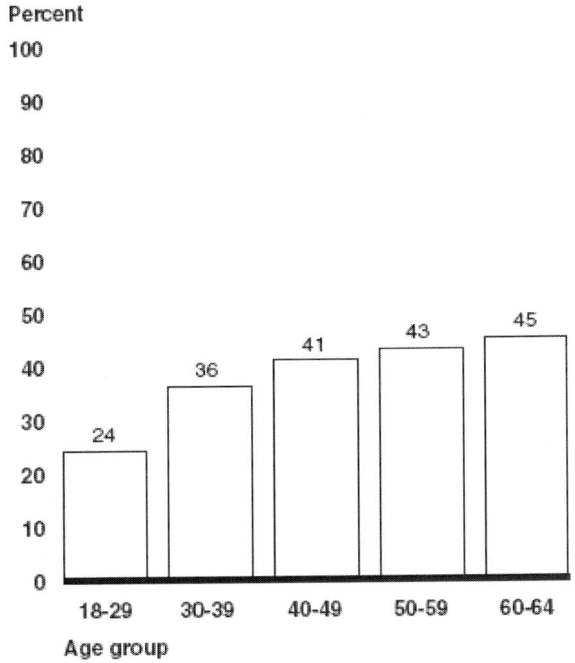

Source: GAO analysis of 2004 Survey of Consumer Finances.

Note: Most SCF percentage estimates have 95 percent confidence intervals between plus-or-minus 4 percentage points of the percentage itself. Exceptions to this rule are presented in app. I.

Figure 2. Percentage of Working Individuals Participating in Current DC Plans by Age Group, 2004.

For many workers who participated in a plan, overall balances in DC plans were modest, suggesting a potentially small contribution toward retirement security for most plan participants and their households. However, since DC plans were less common before the 1980s, older workers would not have had access to these plans their whole careers. In order to approximate lifetime DC balances when discussing mean and median DC balances in this report, our analysis of the 2004 SCF aggregates the "total balances" of DC plans with a current employer, DC plans with former employers that have been left with the former employer, and any retirement plans with former employers that have been rolled over into a new plan or an IRA.[23] Workers with a "current or former DC plan" refers to current workers with one or more of those three components. For all workers with a current or former DC plan, the median total balance was $22,800. For all households with a current or former DC plan, the median total balance was $27,940 (see fig. 3).

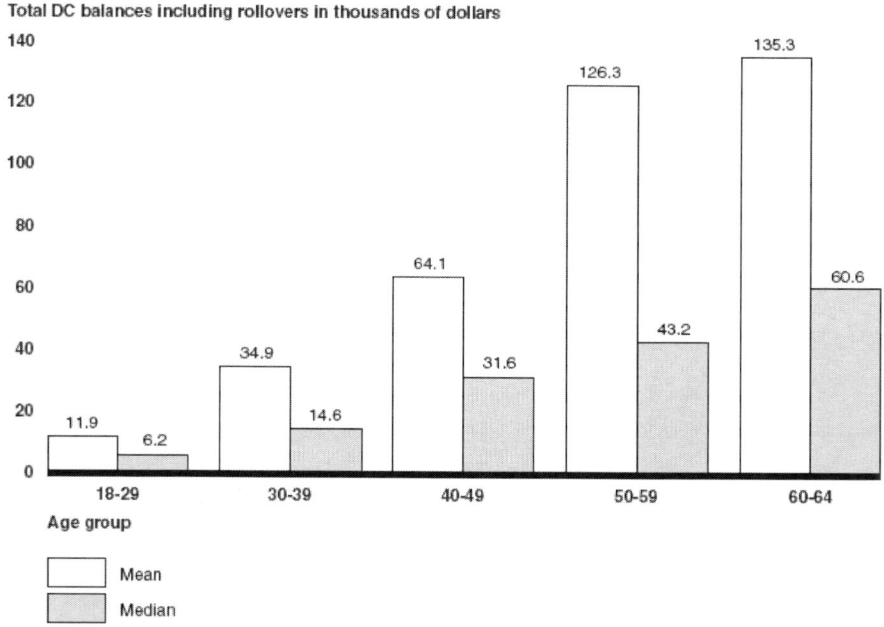

Source: GAO analysis of 2004 Survey of Consumer Finances.

Note: The majority of SCF estimates of medians and means have 95 percent confidence intervals within plus-or-minus 25 percent of the estimate itself. Exceptions to this rule are summarized in app. I.

Figure 3. Total DC Balances for Working Individuals with a Current or Former DC Plan, by Age Group, 2004.

For individuals nearing retirement age, total DC plan balances are still low. Given trends in coverage since the 1980's, older workers close to retirement age are more likely than younger ones to have accrued retirement benefits in a DB plan. However, older workers who will rely on DC plans for retirement income may not have time to substantially increase their total savings without extending their working careers, perhaps for several years. Among all workers aged 55 to 64 with a current or former DC plan, the median balance according to the 2004 SCF was $50,000, which would provide an income of about $4,400 a year, replacing about 9 percent of income for the average worker in this group.[24] Among all workers aged 60 to 64 with a current or former DC plan, the median balance was $60,600 for their accounts. Markedly higher values for mean balances versus median balances in figure 3 illustrate that some individuals in every age group are successfully saving far more than the typical individual, increasing the mean savings. These are primarily individuals at the highest levels of income.

Leakage, or cashing out accumulated retirement savings for non-retirement purposes, adversely affects account accumulation for some of those with accounts, particularly for lower-income workers with small account balances. Participants who withdraw money from a DC plan before age 59 1/2 generally pay ordinary income taxes on the distributions,[25] plus an additional 10 percent tax in most circumstances.[26] Participants may roll their DC plan balances into another tax-preferred account when they leave a job, and employers are required, in the absence of participant direction, to automatically roll DC account distributions greater than $1,000 but not greater than $5,000 into an IRA, or to leave the money in the plan. As of 2004, 21 percent of households in which the head of household was under 59, had ever received lump-sum distributions from previous jobs' retirement plans. Among these households that received lump-sum distributions, 47 percent had cashed out all the funds, 4 percent cashed out some of the funds, and 50 percent preserved all the funds by rolling them over into another retirement account.[27] Workers were more likely to roll over funds when the balances are greater. Among households that had cashed out all retirement plans with former employers, the median total value of those funds was $6,800. For households that had rolled over all retirement plans with former employers, the median total value of rolled-over funds was $24,200.[28]

Some evidence suggests that pre-retirement withdrawals may be decreasing. One study finds that those receiving lump-sum distributions are more likely to preserve funds in tax-qualified accounts than they were in the past.[29] For example, data show that in 1993, 19 percent of lump-sum distributions recipients preserved all of their savings by rolling them into a tax-qualified account, compared to 43 percent in 2003. Further, 23 percent used all of their distribution for consumption in 1993, declining to 15 percent in 2003 (see fig. 4). According to the same study, age and size of the distribution are major determinants of whether or not the distribution is preserved in a tax-qualified account. For example, the authors found 55.5 percent of recipients aged 51 to 60 rolled their entire distribution in a tax-qualified account compared with 32.7 percent of recipients 21 to 30. Additionally, 19.9 percent of distributions from $1 to $499 were rolled over in tax-qualified accounts, as opposed to 68.1 percent of distributions of $50,000 or more.

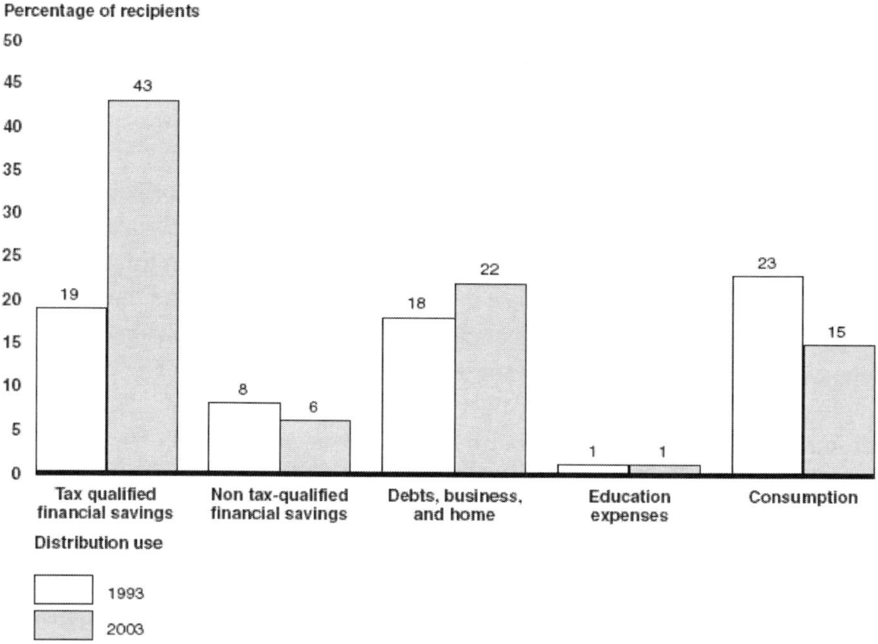

Source: "Lump Sum Distributions" in Employee Benefit Research Institute Notes, Volume 26 Number 12.

Note: EBRI estimates from 2001 Panel of the Survey of Income and Program Participation Topical Module 7, 1996; Panel of the Survey of Income and Program Participation Topical Module 7, and April, 1993 Employee Benefits Supplement to the Current Population Survey.

Figure 4. Portion of Lump-Sum Distribution Recipients Using the Entire Portion of Their Most Recent Distribution, by Use, 1993, and 2003.

Additionally, some participants take loans from their DC plan, which may reduce plan savings. One survey found that in 2005, 85.2 percent of employers surveyed offered a loan option.[30] Most eligible participants do not take loans, and one analysis finds that at years end 2006, loans amounted to 12 percent of account balances for those who had loans.[31] Individuals may prefer to take out pension loans in lieu of other lines of credit because pension loans require no approval and have low or no transaction costs. Borrowers also pay the loan principal and interest back to their own accounts. However, someone borrowing from a DC plan may still lose money if the interest on the loan paid back to the account is less than the account balance would have earned if the loan had not been taken. Further, loans not paid back in time, or not paid back before the employee leaves the job, may be subject to early withdrawal penalties. No data have been reported on the rate of loan defaults, but it is expected to be much lower where repayments are made by payroll withholding. However, a loan feature may also have a positive effect on participation, as some workers may choose to participate who otherwise might not, precisely because they can borrow from their accounts for non-retirement purposes at relatively low interest rates.[32]

Low-Income Workers Have Particularly Low DC Plan Coverage and Plan Balances

Among workers in the lowest income quartile, only 8 percent participated in a current DC plan, a result of markedly lower access as well as lower participation than the average worker (see fig. 5). Only 25 percent of workers in the lowest income quartile were offered any type of retirement plan by their employer, and among those offered a retirement plan, 60 percent elected to participate, compared with 84 percent among workers of all income levels. Workers in the lower half of the income distribution with either current or former DC plans had total median balances of $9,420.

Older workers who were less wealthy also had limited retirement savings. Workers with a current or former DC plan, aged 50-59 and at or below the median level of wealth, had median total savings of only $13,800.[33] Workers with a current or former DC plan, aged 60-64 and at or below the median level of wealth, had median total savings of $18,000, a level that could provide at best only a limited supplement to retirement income. If converted into a single life annuity at age 65, this balance would provide only $132 per month—about $1,600 per year.[34]

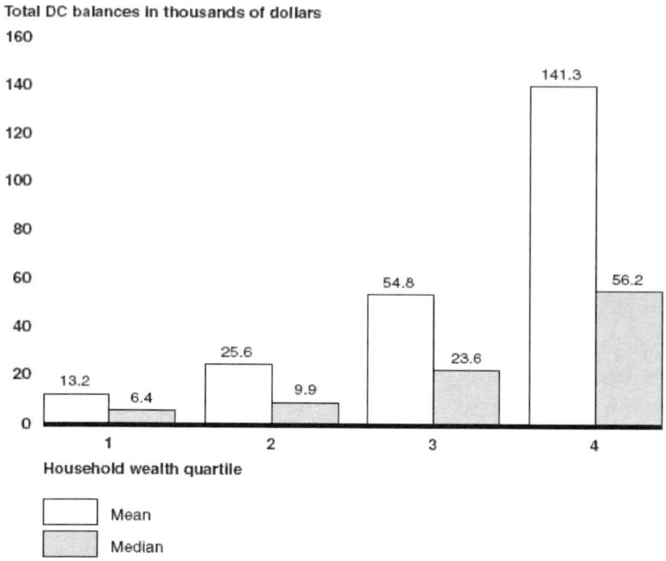

Source: GAO analysis of 2004 Survey of Consumer Finances.

Figure 5. Total DC Plan Balances for Working Individuals with a Current or Former DC Plan, by Household Wealth Quartiles, 2004.

Notably, workers with low DC balances were actually less likely to have a DB pension to fall back on than workers with higher DC balances. Among all workers participating in current or former DC plans, only 17 percent of those in the bottom quartile for total plan savings also were covered by a current DB plan. In contrast, 32 percent of those in the top quartile for total DC savings also had DB coverage. Among all workers with a current or former DC plan, the plan balances for those with DB coverage were higher than for those without DB coverage. The median DC balance for workers with a DB account was $31,560, while the median DC balance for someone without a DB account was $20,820.

PROJECTED DC PLAN SAVINGS ARE SMALL FOR MOST WORKERS, BUT COULD VARY WIDELY DEPENDING ON SEVERAL FACTORS

Simulations of projected retirement savings in DC plans suggest that a large percentage of workers may accumulate enough over their careers to replace only a small fraction of their working income, although results vary widely by income levels and depend on model assumptions. Projected savings allow us to analyze how much workers might save over a full working career under a variety of conditions in a way that analyzing current plan balances cannot, since DC plans have become primary employer-sponsored plans only relatively recently. Baseline simulations of projected retirement savings for a hypothetical 1990 birth cohort indicate that DC plan savings would on average replace about 22 percent of annualized career earnings,[35] but provide no savings to almost 37 percent of the working population, perhaps because of different factors — working for employers who do not offer a plan, choosing not to participate, or withdrawing any accumulated plan savings prior to retirement.[36] Further, projected DC account balances vary widely by income quartile, with workers in the lowest-income quartile saving enough for about a 10 percent replacement rate, while those in the highest quartile saving enough for a 34 percent replacement rate, on average. Assuming changes in certain plan features, individual behavior, or market assumptions, such as increased participation or account rollover rates, increased projected average savings and increased the number of workers who had some DC plan savings at retirement, especially for low-income workers. Other scenarios, such as assuming higher contribution limits or delaying retirement, raised average replacement rates, but with more of the positive impact on higher-income workers and having little effect on reducing the number of workers with no savings at retirement.[37]

Projected DC Plan Balances Vary Widely by Income, with Many Workers Having No Plan Savings at Retirement

Our projections, based on a sample of workers born in 1990, show that workers would save enough in their DC plans over their careers to produce, when converted to a lifetime annuity at the time of retirement, an average of $18,784 per year in 2007 dollars (see table 3).[38] The projections assume that all workers fully annuitize all accumulated DC plans balances at retirement, which occurs sometime between age 62 and 70. Participants are assumed to always invest all plan assets in life cycle funds, and stocks earn an average real annual return of 6.4 percent. This $18,784 annuity would replace, on average, 22.2 percent of annualized career earnings for workers in the cohort. Savings and replacement rates vary widely across income groups. Almost 37 percent of workers in this cohort have no projected DC plan savings at retirement, which brings down overall average replacement rates. Workers in the lowest income quartile accumulate DC plan savings equivalent to an annuity of about $1,850 per year, or a 10.3 percent replacement rate, and 63 percent of this group have no plan savings by the time they retire. In contrast, highest income quartile workers save enough to receive about $50,000 per year in annuity income, enough for a 33.8 percent replacement rate. Even in this highest-income group, over 16 percent of workers have zero plan savings at retirement. In all cases, our replacement rates include projected savings only in DC plans. Retirees may also receive benefits from DB plans, as well as from Social Security, which typically replaces a higher percentage of earnings for lower-income workers.

Projected household-level plan savings show a higher average replacement rate of 33.8 percent, with about 29 percent of households having no plan savings at retirement. When we assume that plan assets earn a lower average real annual return of 2.9 percent, average replacement rates from DC plan savings fall to about 16 percent for the sample.[39] Under this assumption, workers in the lowest-income quartile receive an average 7.1 percent replacement rate from DC plans, while highest-income quartile workers receive an average 25 percent replacement rate. Lower rates of return affect the percentage of workers with no accumulated DC plan savings only slightly, perhaps because on the margins some participants might choose (or have their employers choose) to cash out lower balances.

Table 3 also shows savings statistics for sub-samples of the cohort who have a better chance of accumulating significant DC plan savings, such as those workers who have long-term eligibility to participate in a plan or who work for many years. As expected, these groups have higher projected savings; replacement rates also show more even distribution across income groups, compared to those in the full sample. However, we still see a significant portion of the workers with no DC savings at retirement. First, we limit the sample only to those workers who are eligible to participate in a plan for at least 15 years over their careers. Average replacement rates for this group measure 33.5 percent, with rates ranging from 21.7 percent for lowest income quartile workers to 42.3 percent for the highest quartile.[40] Even with such long-term eligibility for plan coverage, however, 15.6 percent of these workers, and almost one-third of lowest-income workers, have nothing saved in DC plans at the time they retire. This could result from workers choosing not to participate or from cashing out plan balances prior to retirement.

Table 3. Projected Average Annuity Equivalents and Replacement Rates from DC Plan Balances at Retirement, by Income, under Baseline Assumptions

		By income quartile			
Individual-level results	**Overall**	**1**	**2**	**3**	**4**
Annuity equivalent (per year, 2007 dollars)	18,784	1,850	6,554	16,635	50,098
Replacement rate (percent)	22.2	10.3	18.2	26.3	33.8
Percent of workers with no DC savings	36.8	63.0	39.8	27.9	16.4
Household-level results					
Annuity equivalent (per year, 2007 dollars)	24,664	4,176	11,918	25,560	57,000
Replacement rate (percent)	33.8	18.7	30.3	40.9	45.5
Percent of workers with no DC savings	28.8	48.1	30.7	21.8	14.5
Only workers eligible for a DC plan for 15+ years					
Annuity equivalent (per year, 2007 dollars)	29,844	5,133	13,629	30,178	70,437
Replacement rate (percent)	33.5	21.7	30.2	39.7	42.3
Percent of workers with no DC savings	15.6	32.6	16.6	9.1	4.1
Only those working 25+ years full-time					
Annuity equivalent (per year, 2007 dollars)	25,533	4,447	11,407	25,610	60,668
Replacement rate (percent)	26.5	16.3	23.3	31.7	34.9
Percent of workers with no DC savings	28.8	46.7	31.8	22.8	14.5
Assuming 2.9 percent real annual return on stocks					
Annuity equivalent (per year, 2007 dollars)	13,803	1,277	4,687	12,145	37,100
Replacement rate (percent)	16.1	7.1	13.0	19.2	25.1
Percent of workers with no DC savings	37.2	63.3	40.3	28.3	16.7

Source: GAO projections using PENSIM model.

Note: All results are individual level, except as indicated. Model assumptions include the following: 1) workers fully annuitize all accumulated DC plan balances at retirement, between age 62 and 70; 2) participants invest all plan assets in life cycle funds; 3) stocks earn an average annual 6.4 percent real return, except where specified. Replacement rates equal annuitized income from lifetime DC plan savings divided by annualized career earnings. See app. I for more details.

We also analyze the prospects of workers with long-term attachment to the labor market, for which we use people who work full-time for at least 25 years, without regard to plan coverage or participation. Among these workers, average DC plan savings at retirement account for a 26.5 percent replacement rate. Still, almost 29 percent of these workers have no projected savings. This suggests that while DC plans have the potential to provide significant retirement income, saving may be difficult for some workers who work for many years, even among those whose employers offer a plan.

Universal Participation in Sponsored Plans and Universal Account Rollover Raise Projected DC Plan Savings Substantially for Lower-Income Workers

Our simulations indicate that increasing participation and reducing leakage out of DC plans may have a particularly significant impact on overall savings, especially for lower-income workers. Of the changes in the model assumptions that we simulated, these had the broadest effect on savings because they not only raised average savings for the entire sample, but had a relatively strong impact on workers in the lowest income quartile and on the number of workers with no DC plan savings at retirement. While these assumptions represent stylized scenarios, they illustrate the potential effect of such changes on savings.

We project DC plan savings assuming that all employees of a firm that sponsors a DC plan participate immediately, rather than having to wait for eligibility or choosing not to participate.[41] In our baseline projections, 6 percent of workers whose employers sponsor a plan are ineligible to participate, and 33 percent of those eligible do not choose to participate; therefore, this assumption significantly raises plan participation rates among workers. Accordingly, average DC savings rise by almost 40 percent, raising average replacement rates to 35 percent, and the percentage of the population with no savings at retirement drops by half, down to 17.7 percent (see table 4).

Assuming automatic eligibility and participation raises projected plan savings significantly for lower-wage workers, more than doubling the annuity equivalent of retirement savings for the lowest-income quartile. Workers in the highest income group also increase savings under this scenario, with plan savings rising by 30 percent. This change in projected savings suggests that automatically enrolling new employees in plans as a default could have a significant positive impact on DC balances, especially for low-income workers whose jobs offer a plan, although this stylized scenario likely describes a more extreme change in eligibility and participation than plans are likely to implement under automatic enrollment, and that higher participation and savings would raise employer's pension costs, perhaps leading to a reduction in benefits or coverage.

Table 4. Projected Average Annuity Equivalents and Replacement Rates from DC Plan Balances at Retirement, by Income, under Different Model Assumptions

		By income quartile			
Baseline results, individual-level	**Overall**	**1**	**2**	**3**	**4**
Annuity equivalent (per year, 2007 dollars)	18,784	1,850	6,554	16,635	50,098
Replacement rate (percent)	22.2	10.3	18.2	26.3	33.8
Percent of workers with no DC savings	36.8	63.0	39.8	27.9	16.4
Instant eligibility/participation					
Annuity equivalent (per year, 2007 dollars)	26,265	4,243	11,142	24,370	65,305
Replacement rate (percent)	35.0	25.4	31.3	38.8	44.7
Percent of workers with no DC savings	17.7	30.0	18.4	13.7	8.6
Participants always roll over balances upon job separation					
Annuity equivalent (per year, 2007 dollars)	20,797	2,428	7,892	18,949	53,918
Replacement rate (percent)	25.6	13.8	22.0	30.1	36.6
Percent of workers with no DC savings	27.0	48.8	28.1	19.3	11.6

Source: GAO projections using PENSIM model.

Note: All results are individual level. Model assumptions include the following: 1) workers fully annuitize all accumulated DC plan balances at retirement, between age 62 and 70; 2) participants invest all plan assets in life cycle funds; 3) stocks earn an average annual 6.4 percent real return, except where specified. Replacement rates equal annuitized income from lifetime DC plan savings divided by annualized career earnings. See app. I for more details.

Another stylized scenario we model assumes that all workers who have a DC plan balance always keep the money in a tax-preferred account upon leaving a job, either by keeping the money in the plan, transferring it to a new employer plan, or rolling it into an IRA, rather than cashing out any accumulated savings.[42] Eliminating this source of leakage raises average annuity income from DC plans by almost 11 percent and average replacement rates from 22.2 percent in the baseline to 25.6 percent; it also reduces the percentage of the cohort with no DC savings at retirement by over 25 percent. As with the instant participation scenario, "universal rollover" raises annuity savings and reduces the number of retirees with zero plan savings by the biggest percentages among lower-income workers, suggesting that cashing out accumulate plan savings prior to retirement may be a more significant drain on retirement savings for these groups. These results indicate that policies to encourage participants to keep DC plan balances in tax-preferred retirement accounts, perhaps by making rollover of plan assets a default action in plans, may have a broad positive impact on retirement savings.

Changing Retirement Decisions or Contribution Limits Would Affect Savings Primarily for Higher-Income Workers

Other changes we make in our projections related to plan features or individual behavior affect average replacement rates overall, but with less impact on lower-income workers' replacement rates and on the number of workers with zero plan savings at retirement. These scenarios include assumed changes in annual contribution limits and retirement decisions (see table 5).

We model projected retirement savings assuming that annual DC contribution limits for employees rise from $15,500 to $25,000, and the combined employer-employee maximum contribution level rises from $45,000 to $60,000, starting in 2007.[43] Higher annual maximum contributions affect projected savings almost exclusively among the highest-income group, indicating that few workers earning less are likely to contribute at existing maximum levels. The highest income quartile replacement rises from 33.8 to 38.5 percent, while replacement rates hardly change in the lower income groups. Similarly, this scenario has almost no impact on the percentage of workers with DC plan savings at retirement.

Table 5. Projected Average Annuity Equivalents and Replacement Rates from DC Plan Balances at Retirement, by Income, under Different Model Assumptions

Baseline results, individual-level			By income quartile		
	Overall	1	2	3	4
Annuity equivalent (per year, 2007 dollars)	18,784	1,850	6,554	16,635	50,098
Replacement rate (percent)	22.2	10.3	18.2	26.3	33.8
Percent of workers with no DC savings	36.8	63.0	39.8	27.9	16.4
Raise annual contribution limits					
Annuity equivalent (per year, 2007 dollars)	21,056	1,879	6,583	16,999	58,763
Replacement rate (percent)	23.6	10.5	18.3	26.9	38.5
Percent of workers with no DC savings	36.7	63.0	39.9	27.9	16.2
Workers delay retirement 1 year					
Annuity equivalent (per year, 2007 dollars)	19,873	1,876	6,895	17,826	52,895
Replacement rate (percent)	23.3	10.5	19.0	28.0	35.6
Percent of workers with no DC savings	36.9	63.5	40.3	27.2	16.3
Workers delay retirement 3 years					
Annuity equivalent (per year, 2007 dollars)	22,710	2,151	7,623	19,897	61,170
Replacement rate (percent)	25.7	12.1	20.7	30.5	39.4
Percent of workers with no DC savings	36.8	63.1	39.9	28.5	15.7

Source: GAO calculations using projected savings from PENSIM model.

Note: All results are individual level. Model assumptions include the following: 1) workers fully annuitize all accumulated DC plan balances at retirement, between age 62 and 70; 2) participants invest all plan assets in life cycle funds; 3) stocks earn an average annual 6.4 percent real return, except where specified. Replacement rates equal annuitized income from lifetime DC plan savings divided by annualized career earnings. See app. I for more details.

Finally, we model retirement savings in two scenarios in which workers delay retirement by 1 or 3 years. Encouraging workers to retire later has been suggested as a key element in improving retirement income security, by increasing earnings, allowing more time to save for retirement, and reducing the length of retirement. In our projections, delaying retirement not only provides more years to contribute to and earn returns on plan balances but also might raise annual retirement income because older retirees receive more annuity income for any given level of savings, holding all else equal. In our projections, working longer modestly raises retirement savings in our projections. Working one extra year changes projected annuity income by 5.8 percent, but has little effect on the percentage of people with no DC savings in our projections. Delaying retirement by 3 years raises annuity income from DC plans by 20.9 percent on average, with replacement rates rising from 22.2 percent in the baseline to 25.7 percent overall.[44] The 3-year delay increases annuity levels somewhat evenly across income groups, with higher-income workers showing slightly higher increases. Overall, working an extra 3 years raises average replacement rates about as much as universal account rollover would, but with little reduction in workers with no retirement savings. Thus, while working longer would likely raise workers' incomes, and in most cases retirement benefits from other sources such as Social Security, our projections show that this change alone would have a modest impact on retirement income from DC plans, particularly regarding lower-income workers and those not already saving in DC plans in the baseline.

Recent Changes and Proposals Could Have Positive Effects on DC Plan Coverage, Participation, and Savings

Recent regulatory and legislative changes and proposals could have positive effects on DC plan coverage, participation, and saving. The Pension Protection Act of 2006 (PPA) facilitated the adoption of automatic plan features by plan sponsors that may increase DC participation and savings within existing plans.[45] Proposals to expand the saver's credit could similarly encourage greater contributions by low-wage workers who are already covered by a DC plan. Other options, like the so-called "State-K" proposal, in which states would design and partner with private financial institutions to offer low-cost DC plans employers could provide to employees, would seek to expand coverage among workers without current plans by encouraging employers to sponsor new plans. Other options would try to increase retirement account coverage by increasing the use of IRAs or creating new retirement savings vehicles outside of the voluntary employer-sponsored pension framework. Such proposals include automatic IRAs, in which employers would be required to allow employees through automatic enrollment to contribute to IRAs by direct payroll deposit, or universal accounts proposals, in which all workers would be given a retirement account regardless of whether they had any employment based pension coverage.

Changing Default Plan Features and Reforming Saver's Credit Could Raise DC Plan Savings, but May Have Limited Impact on Coverage

Changing certain traditional DC plan defaults may have a significant impact on DC participation and savings. Research suggests that employees exhibit inertia regarding plan participation and contributions, which can reduce DC savings by failure to participate or increase savings over time.[46] To reverse the effects of these tendencies, some experts have suggested changing default plan actions to automatically sign up employees for participation, escalate contributions, and set default investment options unless workers opt out.[47] Some studies have shown that automatic enrollment may increase DC plan participation. For example, one study of a large firm, automatic enrollment increased participation from 57 percent for employees eligible to participate 1 year before the firm adopted automatic enrollment to 86 percent for those hired under automatic enrollment.[48] Another study finds that, prior to automatic enrollment, 26 to 43 percent of employees at 6 months' tenure participated in the plan at three different companies; under automatic enrollment 86 to 96 percent of employees participated.[49] Some also advocate automatically rolling over DC savings into an IRA when employees separate from their employers to further increase retirement savings. Our own simulations shows that universal account rollover to a tax-preferred account, such as a new plan or an IRA, would increase projected retirement savings by 11 percent on average, with the biggest percentage increases for lowest-income workers.

Various regulatory and legislative changes have focused on default DC plan features. In 1998, the IRS first approved plan sponsor use of automatic enrollment—the ability for plans to automatically sign employees up for a 401(k) plan (from which the employee can opt out), and—subsequently issued several rulings that clarified the use of other automatic plan features and the permissibility of automatic features in 403(b) and 457 plans.[50] Accordingly, the percentage of 401(k) plans using automatic plan features has increased in recent years. One annual study of plan sponsors found that in 2004, 12.4 percent of 401(k) plans were automatically enrolling participants, and this number increased to 17.5 percent of plans in 2005.[51] The percentage of plans automatically increasing employee contributions also rose from 6.8 percent in 2004 to 13.6 percent in 2005. Some experts have argued that initially, some plan sponsors may have been hesitant to use automatic plan features because of legal ambiguities between state and federal law. However, clarifications relating to automatic enrollment and default investment in the PPA have led some plan sponsors and experts to expect more plans to adopt automatic plan features.[52]

Automatic DC plan features, however, may create complications for sponsors and participants that may limit any effect on savings and participation. Auto enrollment may not help expand plan sponsorship; in fact, sponsors who offer a matching contribution may not want to offer automatic enrollment if they believe this will raise their pension costs.[53] Also, if sponsors automatically invest contributions in a low-risk fund such as a money market fund, this could limit rates of return on balances. However, choosing a risky investment fund could subject automatic contributions to market losses.[54] Some employees may not realize they have been signed up for a plan, and may be displeased to discover this, particularly if their automatically invested contributions have lost money.[55]

Proposals Seek to Increase Plan Coverage and Savings, Particularly for Lower-Income Workers

Other proposals would target plan formation or increase participation and retirement savings by expanding worker access to other account-based retirement savings vehicles like IRAs. Some of these alternative retirement savings proposals are voluntary in design, while others are more universal.

State-K: The State-K proposal aims to make low-cost retirement plans available to employers who do not otherwise sponsor a plan.[56] Under a State-K program, state government entities would design and administer a 401(k) plan that an employer within the state could choose to offer its employees. By pooling resources and sharing costs across many different employers, states would seek to create a lower-cost plan that employers, particularly smaller ones, that do not sponsor any plan might find attractive enough to adopt and offer to their employees. In one proposed program from Maryland, expenses to implement, maintain, and administer the plan would be paid from contributions to, or income or assets of, the program.[57] The 401(k) designs made available by a State-K program would use automatic enrollment and low-cost default investment, with limited and simple features to minimize administrative costs and simplify choices for employers and employees. Contributions accumulated by these State-K funds would be kept separate from state employee retirement plan funds, but State-K funds could be pooled in order to lower overall plan investment costs. By decreasing the costs and assisting small employers with compliance and plan administration, the State-K could be expected to increase incentives for employers to sponsor plans, thus increasing employee access to account-based retirement plans. However, it is unclear to what extent employers would adopt such plans.

The Automatic IRA: The Automatic IRA proposal would make direct deposit or payroll deduction saving into an IRA available to all employees by requiring employers that do not sponsor any retirement plan to offer withholding to facilitate employee contributions. To maximize participation, employees would be automatically enrolled at 3 percent of pay, or could elect to opt out or to defer a different percentage of pay to an IRA, up to the maximum IRA annual contribution limit ($4,000 for 2007; $5,000 for 2008). Employers would not be required choose investments or set up the IRAs, which would be provided mainly by the private-sector IRA trustees and custodians that currently provide them. Employers also would not be required or permitted to make matching contributions, and would not need to comply with the Employee Retirement Income Security Act of 1974 (ERISA) or any qualified plan standards such as nondiscrimination requirements. Employers, however, would be required to provide notice to employees, including information on the maximum amount that can be contributed to the plan on an annual basis.[58] One congressional proposal would require employers, other than small or new ones, to offer payroll deposit IRA arrangements to employees not eligible for pension plans and permit automatic enrollment in such IRAs in many circumstances. Participating IRAs would be required to offer a default investment consisting of life cycle funds similar to those offered by the Thrift Savings Plan, the DC plan for federal workers, or other investments specified by a new entity established for that purpose. [59]

Universal accounts: Similar to the automatic IRA, universal account (UA) proposals aim to establish retirement savings accounts for all workers, and vary slightly based on employment-based pension access. Additionally, some proposals would have employers contribute to the account, whereas other proposals would also have the federal government match contributions. One proposal suggests a 2 percent annual contribution from the federal government regardless of individual contributions, while another would provide for individual contributions only, capped at $7,500 per year.[60] In 1999, the Clinton Administration proposed a UA to be established for each worker and spouse with earnings of at least $5,000 annually. Individuals would receive a tax credit of up to $300 annually. Additionally, workers could voluntarily contribute to the account up to specified amounts with a 50 to 100 percent match by the federal government.[61] This match would come in the form of a tax credit, and total voluntary contributions, including government contributions, would be limited to $1,000. Both the credit and the match would phase out as income increases, providing a progressive benefit and targeting low- and middle-income workers. Federal contributions would have revenue implications, while requiring employer contributions could increase employer compensation costs.

Other proposals would expand the size and scope of the saver's credit to encourage greater contributions by those low-wage workers who are already covered by a DC plan that allows employee contributions. Currently, the saver's credit, originally proposed in 2000 as an outgrowth of the 1999 UA proposal as a government matching deposit on some voluntary contributions to IRAs and 401(k) plans, provides a nonrefundable tax credit to low- and middle-income savers of up to 50 percent of their annual IRA or 401(k) contributions of up to $2,000. However, according to one analysis, because the credit is nonrefundable, only about 17 percent of those with incomes low enough to qualify for the credit would receive any benefit if they contributed to a plan. Some analysts think that expanding the saver's credit, or creating direct transfers such as tax rebates or deposits into retirement savings accounts, could increase plan contributions specifically for low- and middle-income workers.[62] Making the saver's credit refundable to the participant could also provide a direct transfer to the tax filer in lieu of a retirement account match, but offers no assurance that funds would be saved or deposited into a retirement account.[63] A refundable tax credit would also have revenue implications for the federal budget.

CONCLUDING OBSERVATIONS

The DC plan has clearly overtaken the DB plan as the principal retirement plan for the nation's private sector workforce, and its growing dominance suggests its increasingly crucial role in the retirement security of current and future generations of workers. The current DC-based system faces major challenges, like its DB-based predecessor, in terms of coverage, participation, and lifetime distributions. Achieving retirement security through DC plans carries particular challenges for workers, since accumulating benefits in an account-based plan requires more active commitment and management from individuals than it does for DB participants. Since workers must typically sign up and voluntarily reduce their take home pay to contribute to their DC plans, invest this money wisely over their working years, and resist withdrawing from balances prior to retirement, it is perhaps to be expected that even those who have the opportunity to participate save little. While our results on both current and projected plan balances suggest that while some workers save significant amounts toward their retirement in DC plans, a large proportion of workers will likely not save enough in DC plans for a secure retirement.

Of particular concern are the retirement income challenges faced by lower earners. Many of these workers face competing income demands for basic necessities that may make contributions to their retirement plans difficult. Further, the tax preferences that may entice higher-income workers to contribute to their DC plans may not entice low-income workers who have plan coverage, since these workers face relatively low marginal tax rates. Our model results suggest that other measures, such as automatic enrollment and rollover of funds may make a difference for some lower income workers. Should pension policy, as embodied by the automatic provisions in PPA, continue to move in this direction, it should focus on those workers most in need of enhanced retirement income prospects.

AGENCY COMMENTS

We provided a draft of this report to the Department of Labor and the Department of the Treasury, as well as to five outside reviewers. Neither agency provided formal comments. We incorporated any technical comments we received throughout the report as appropriate.

Sincerely yours,

Barbara D. Bovbjerg
Director
Education, Workforce, and Income Security Issues

APPENDIX I: SCOPE AND METHODOLOGY

To analyze saving in DC plans, we examined data from the Federal Reserve Board's Survey of Consumer Finances (SCF). This triennial survey asks extensive questions about household income and wealth components. We used the latest available survey, from 2004. The SCF is widely used by the research community, is continually vetted by the Federal Reserve and users, and is considered to be a reliable data source. The SCF is believed by many to be the best source of publicly available information on household finances. Further information about our use of the SCF, including sampling errors, as well as definitions and assumptions we made in our analysis are detailed below. We also reviewed published statistics in articles by public policy groups and in academic studies.

To analyze how much Americans can expect to save in DC plans over their careers and the factors that affect these savings, we used the Policy Simulation Group's (PSG) microsimulation models to run various simulations of workers saving over a working career, changing various inputs to model different scenarios that affect savings at retirement. PENSIM is a pension policy simulation model that has been developed for the Department of Labor to analyze lifetime coverage and adequacy issues related to employer-sponsored pensions in the United States. We projected account balances at retirement for PENSIM-generated workers under different scenarios representing different pension features, individual behavioral decisions, and market assumptions. See below for further discussion of PENSIM and our assumptions and methodologies.

To analyze those plan- or government-level policies that might best increase participation and savings in DC plans, we synthesized information gathered from interviews of plan practitioners, financial managers, and public policy experts, as well as from academic and policy studies on DC plan participation and savings. We also researched current government initiatives and policy proposals to broaden participation in account-based pension plans and increase retirement savings.

We conducted our work from July 2006 to October 2007 in accordance with generally accepted government auditing standards.

Methodology and Assumptions Using Survey of Consumer Finances Data

The 2004 SCF surveyed 4,522 households about their pensions, incomes, labor force participation, asset holdings and debts, use of financial services, and demographic information. The SCF is conducted using a dual-frame sample design. One part of the design is a standard, multi-stage area-probability design, while the second part is a special oversample of relatively wealthy households. This is done in order to accurately capture financial information about the population at large as well as characteristics specific to the relatively wealthy. The two parts of the sample are adjusted for sample nonresponse and combined using weights to provide a representation of households overall. In addition, the SCF excludes people included in the Forbes Magazine list of the 400 wealthiest people in the United States. Furthermore, the 2004 SCF dropped three observations from the public data set that had net worth at least equal to the minimum level needed to qualify for the Forbes list.

The SCF is a probability sample based on random selections, so the 2004 SCF sample is only one of a large number of samples that might have been drawn. Since each sample could have provided different estimates, we express our confidence in the precision of our particular sample's results as a 95 percent confidence interval (e.g., plus or minus 4 percentage points). This is the interval that would contain the actual population value for 95 percent of the samples we could have drawn. As a result, we are 95 percent confident that each of the confidence intervals in this report will include the true values in the study population.

All percentage estimates based on GAO analysis of 2004 SCF data used in this report have 95 percent confidence intervals that are within plus-orminus 4 percentage points, with the following exceptions described in table 6 below.

Table 6. Sampling Errors Greater than 4 Percentage Points for Percentage Estimates at the 95 Percent Confidence Interval

Estimate	Value	Sampling error
Percentage of workers aged 60-64 participating in current DC plans	45	+/- 7.6
Percentage of households who had previously received lump-sum distributions who cashed out all funds	47	+/- 4.7
Percentage of households who had previously received lump-sum distributions who rolled over all funds	50	+/- 4.3
Percentage of workers, in the lowest income quartile and offered a retirement plan, participating in current DC plans	60	+/- 5.8

Source: GAO analysis of 2004 SCF data.

Other numerical estimates based on GAO analysis of 2004 SCF data used in this report have 95 percent confidence intervals that are within 25 percent of the estimate itself, with exceptions described in table 7. [1]

Table 7. Sampling Errors Greater Than 25 Percent for Numerical Estimates at the 95 Percent Confidence Interval

	Estimate (2003dollars)	Sampling error (Plus or minus)
Median total DC balances for all workers with either a current or former DC plan	24,200	+/-5,303
Median total DC balances for all households with either a current or former DC plan	27,940	+/-4,762
Median total DC balances for workers with either a current or former DC plan (aged 18-29)	6,160	+/-3,791
Median total DC balances for workers with either a current or former DC plan (aged 30-39)	14,580	+/-2,852
Median total DC balances for workers with either a current or former DC plan (aged 40-49)	31,580	+/-7,460
Median total DC balances for workers with either a current or former DC plan (aged 50-59)	43,200	+/-12,113
Median total DC balances for workers with either a current or former DC plan (aged 60-64)	60,600	+/-23,435

	Estimate (2003dollars)	Sampling error (Plus or minus)
Mean total DC balances for workers with either a current or former DC plan (aged 18-29)	11,865	+/-2,507
Mean total DC balances for workers with either a current or former DC plan (aged 30-39)	34,851	+/-6,507
Mean total DC balances for workers with either a current or former DC plan (aged 40-49)	64,124	+/-8,271
Mean total DC balances for workers with either a current or former DC plan (aged 50-59)	126,301	+/-25,156
Mean total DC balances for workers with either a current or former DC plan (aged 60-64)	135,299	+/-34,933
Median total DC balances for workers with either a current or former DC plan (aged 55-64)	50,000	+/-22,406
Median Total of Cashed Out Funds for households that cashed out all lump sum distributions	6,800	+/-1,429
Median Total of Rolled Over Funds for households that rolled over all lump sum distributions	24,200	+/-5,303
Median total DC balances for workers of median income or lower with either a current or former DC plan	9,420	+/-2,165
Median total DC balances for workers of median wealth or lower with either a current or former DC plan (aged 50-59)	13,800	+/-5,244
Median total DC balances for workers of median wealth or lower with either a current or former DC plan (aged 60-64)	18,000	+/-14,766
Median total DC balances for workers with either a current or former DC plan (with a DB plan)	20,820	+/-2,652
Median total DC balances for workers with either a current or former DC plan (without a DB plan)	31,560	+/-7,640

Source: GAO analysis of 2004 SCF data.

Note: We calculated monthly and yearly incomes as annuity equivalents using the Thrift Savings Plan calculator (http://calc.tsp.gov), assuming an interest rate of 5.250 percent, single life benefits beginning at age 65, no joint survivor benefits, and level payments.

Because of the complexity of the SCF design and the need to suppress some detailed sample design information to maintain confidentiality of respondents, standard procedures for estimate of sampling errors could not be used. Further, the SCF uses multiple imputations to estimate responses to most survey questions to which respondents did not provide answers. Sampling error estimates for this report are based on a bootstrap technique using replicate weights to produce estimates of sampling error that account for both the variability due to sampling and due to imputation.[2]

The SCF collects detailed information about an economically dominant single individual or couple in a household (what the SCF calls a primary economic unit), where the individuals are at least 18 years old. We created an additional sample containing information on 7,471 individuals by separating information about respondents and their spouses or partners and considering them separately. When we discuss individuals in this document, we are referring to this sample. When we refer to all workers, we are referring to the subpopulation of workers within this individual sample. In households where there are additional adult workers, beyond the respondent and the spouse or partner, who may also have earnings and a retirement plan, information about these additional workers is not captured by the SCF and is therefore not part of our analysis. It is also important to note that the SCF was designed to be used as a household survey, and some information could not be broken into individual-level information. Where that was the case, we presented only household-level information.

We defined "worker" relatively broadly and opted to begin with the set of all those who reported that they were both working and some other activity, including for example, "worker plus disabled" and "worker plus retired." We then excluded those workers who reported that they were self-employed from our analysis. Our definition of DC plans includes the following plans: 401(k); 403(b); 457; thrift/savings plan; profit-sharing plan; portable cash option plan; deferred compensation plan, n.e.c.; SEP/SIMPLE; money purchase plan; stock purchase plan; and employee stock ownership plan (ESOP).

The SCF and other surveys that are based on self-reported data are subject to several other sources of nonsampling error, including the inability to get information about all sample cases; difficulties of definition; differences in the interpretation of questions; respondents' inability or unwillingness to provide correct information; and errors made in collecting, recording, coding, and processing data. These nonsampling errors can influence the accuracy of information presented in the report, although the magnitude of their effect is not known.

Our analysis of the 2004 SCF yielded slightly lower participation rates than other data sets that consider pensions. For example, 2004 Bureau of Labor Statistics (BLS) data indicate a somewhat higher rate of active participation in DC accounts, 42 percent, compared with our finding of 36 percent. One possible factor contributing to this difference is that BLS surveys establishments about their employees, while SCF surveys individuals who report on themselves and their households; it is possible that the SCF respondents may be failing to report all retirement accounts, while BLS is capturing a greater proportion of them. Also, the SCF considered both public and private sector workers, while the BLS statistic is only for private sector workers. Differences may also be explained by different definitions of workers and participation, question wording, or lines of questioning. The SCF appears to provide a lower bound on the estimation of pension coverage among 4 major data sets.[3]

Methodology and Assumptions Using PENSIM Microsimulation Model

To project lifetime savings in DC pensions, and related retirement plans with personal accounts, and to identify the effects of changes in policies, market assumptions, or individual behavior, we used the Policy Simulation Group's (PSG) Pension Simulator (PENSIM) microsimulation models.[4] PENSIM is a dynamic microsimulation model that produces life histories for a sample of individuals born in the same year.[5] The life history for a sample individual includes different life events, such as birth, schooling events, marriage and divorce, childbirth, immigration and emigration, disability onset and recovery, and death. In addition, a simulated life history includes a complete employment record for each individual, including each job's starting date, job characteristics, pension coverage and plan characteristics, and ending date. The model has been developed by PSG since 1997 with funding and input by the Office of Policy and Research at the Employee Benefits Security Administration (EBSA) of the U.S. Department of Labor with the recommendations of the National Research Council panel on retirement income modeling.

PENSIM sets the timing for each life event by using data from various longitudinal data sets to estimate a waiting-time model (often called a hazard function model) using standard survival analysis methods. PENSIM incorporates many such estimated waiting-time models into a single dynamic simulation model. This model can be used to simulate a synthetic sample of complete life histories. PENSIM employs continuous-time, discrete-event simulation techniques, such that life events do not have to occur at discrete intervals, such as annually on a person's birthday. PENSIM also uses simulated data generated by another PSG simulation model, SSASIM, which produces simulated macro-demographic and macroeconomic variables.

PENSIM imputes pension characteristics using a model estimated with 1996 to 1998 establishment data from the BLS Employee Benefits Survey (now known as the National Compensation Survey). Pension offerings are calibrated to historical trends in pension offerings from 1975 to 2005, including plan mix, types of plans, and employer matching. Further, PENSIM incorporates data from the 1996-1998 Employee Benefits Survey (EBS) to impute access to and participation rates in DC plans in which the employer makes no contribution, which BLS does not report as pension plans in the NCS. The inclusion of these "zero-matching" plans enhances PENSIM's ability to accurately reflect the universe of pension plans offered by employers. PENSIM assumes that 2005 pension offerings, included the imputed zero-matching plans, are projected forward in time.

PSG has conducted validation checks of PENSIM's simulated life histories against both historical life history statistics and other projections. Different life history statistics have been validated against data from the Survey of Income and Program Participation (SIPP), the Current Population Survey (CPS), Modeling Income in the Near Term (MINT3), the Panel Study of Income Dynamics (PSID), and the Social Security Administration's Trustees Report. PSG reports that PENSIM life histories have produced similar annual population, taxable earnings, and disability benefits for the years 2000 to 2080 as those produced by the Congressional Budget Office's long-term social security model (CBOLT) and as shown in the Social Security Administration's 2004 Trustees Report. According to PSG, PENSIM generates simulated DC plan participation rates and account balances that are similar to those observed in a variety of data sets. For example, measures of central tendency in the simulated distribution of DC account balances among employed individuals is similar to those produced by an analysis of the Employee Benefit Research Institute (EBRI)-Investment Company Institute (ICI) 401(k) database and of the 2004 SCF. GAO performed no independent validation checks of PENSIM's life histories or pension characteristics.

In 2006, EBSA submitted PENSIM to a peer review by three economists. The economists' overall reviews ranged from highly favorable to highly critical. While the economist who gave PENSIM a favorable review expressed a "high degree of confidence" in the model, the one who criticized it focused on PENSIM's reduced form modeling. This means that the model is grounded in previously observed statistical relationships among individuals' characteristics, circumstances, and behaviors, rather than on any underlying theory of the determinants of behaviors, such as the common economic theory that individuals make rational choices as their preferences dictate and thereby maximize their own welfare. The third reviewer raised questions about specific modeling assumptions and possible overlooked indirect effects.

Assumptions Used in Projecting DC Plan Balances at Retirement

PENSIM allows the user to alter one or more inputs to represent changes in government policy, market assumptions, or personal behavioral choices and analyze the subsequent impact on pension benefits. Starting with a 2 percent sample of a 1990 cohort, totaling 104,435 people at birth. our baseline simulation includes some of the following key assumptions and features. For our report, we focus exclusively on accumulated balances in DC plans and ignore any benefits an individual might receive from DB plans or from Social Security. Our reported benefits and replacement rates therefore capture just one source of potential income available to a retiree.

- Workers accumulate DC pension benefits from past jobs in one rollover account, which continue to receive investment returns, along with any benefits from a current job. At retirement, these are combined into one account. Because we focus on DC plan balances only, we assume all workers are ineligible to participate in DB plans and do not track Social Security benefits.
- Plan participants invest all assets in their account in life cycle funds, which adjust the mix of assets between stocks and government bonds as the individual ages. Stocks return an annual nonstochastic real rate of return of 6.4 percent and government bonds have a real return of 2.9 percent per year. In one simulation, we use the government bond rate on all plan assets.[6] Using different rates of return reflect assumptions used by OCACT in some of its analyses of trust fund investment.
- Workers purchase a single, nominal life annuity, typically at retirement, which occurs between the ages of 62 and 70. Anyone who

becomes permanently disabled at age 45 or older also purchases an immediate annuity at their disability age.[7] We eliminate from the sample cohort members who: 1) die before they retire, at whatever age; 2) die prior to age 55; 3) immigrates into the cohort at an age older than 25; or 4) becomes permanently disabled prior to age 45. [8] We assume that the annuity provider charges an administrative load on the annuity such that in all scenarios the provider's revenues balance the annuity costs (i.e., zero profit).

- Replacement rates equal the annuity value of DC plan balances divided by a "steady earnings" index. This index reflects career earnings, calibrated to the Social Security Administration's age-65 average wage index (AWI). PENSIM computes steady earnings by first computing the present value of lifetime wages. Then, it calculates a scaling factor that, when multiplied by the present value of lifetime earnings for a 1990 cohort member earning the AWI from ages 21 to 65, produces the individual's present value of lifetime earnings. This scaling factor is multiplied by AWI at age 65, then adjusted to 2007 dollars. Using this measure as opposed to average pay for an individual's final 3 or 5 years of working, minimizes the problems presented by a worker who has irregular earnings near the end of his or her career, perhaps because of reduced hours.[9]
- For household replacement rates, we use a combined annuity value of worker-spouse lifetime DC plan savings and a combined measure of steady family earnings.

Starting from this baseline model, we vary key inputs and assumptions to see how these variations affect pension benefits and replacement rates at retirement. Scenarios we ran include:

1) **Universal rollover of DC plan balances**. All workers with a DC balance roll it over into an Individual Retirement Account or another qualified plan upon job separation, as opposed to cashing out the balance, in which case the money is assumed lost for retirement purposes.
2) **Immediate eligibility and participation in a plan**. A worker who would be offered a plan has no eligibility waiting period and immediately enrolls. This does not necessarily mean that the participant makes immediate or regular contributions; contribution

levels are determined stochastically by PENSIM based on worker characteristics.

3) **Delayed retirement**. Workers work beyond the retirement age determined by PENSIM in the baseline run. In one scenario, workers work up to one extra year; in another, they delay retirement for up to 3 years, although 70 remains the maximum retirement age.
4) **Raised contribution limits**. We set annual contribution limits starting in 2007 to $25,000 per individual, up from $15,500 under current law, and $60,000 for combined employer-employee contributions, up from $45,000 under current law. These limits rise with cost of living changes in subsequent years, as is the case in our baseline model.

PENSIM Cohort Summary and Cross-Sectional Statistics

Lifetime summary statistics of the simulated 1990 cohort's workforce and demographic variables give some insight into the model's projected DC savings at retirement that we report (see tables 8 and 9). The 78,045 people in the sample who have some earnings, do not immigrate into the cohort after age 25, live to age 55, and retire (or become disabled at age 45 or older), work a median 29.4 years full-time and 2.1 part-time, with median "steady" earnings of $46,122 (in 2007 dollars).[10] Those whose earnings fall in the lowest quartile work full-time for only a median 14.1 years, while working part-time for 9.1 years, and 13.4 years for their longest-tenured job; this group's median annual steady earnings measure $16,820. In contrast, those in the highest-quartile of earnings work for a median 34.8 years, including 19.5 years for their longest job, and have median steady earnings of $126,380 per year. The results also show that pension coverage varies somewhat across income groups. About 83 percent of workers in the lowest income quartile have at least one job in which they are covered by a DC plan throughout their working careers, and are eligible for DC plan coverage for a median 9.4 years. In contrast, at least 90 percent of workers in the highest three income quartiles have some DC coverage during their careers. Those in the highest income quartile are eligible for DC participation for a median 25.2 years throughout their career.

Table 8. Summary Statistics, PENSIM 1990 Cohort

		By income quartile			
		1	2	3	4
Demographic variables, full sample	Full sample				
N, full sample	104,435				
N, for replacement rate calculations[a]	78,045	19,511	19,511	19,512	19,511
Percent female	49.5	73.8	55.6	44.8	28.2
Education (median)	Some college	High school graduate	High school graduate	Some college	College graduate
Percent who work for at least one DC sponsor during career	90.4	83.2	90.8	92.7	95.1
Percent whose longest-held job offered DC pension	73.3	56.3	71.7	79.2	86.2

Source: GAO calculations of PENSIM simulation of 1990 cohort.

Note: Percentage female and education medians are for entire sample; all other statistics are for only those used in the replacement rate calculations.

[a]Excludes cohort members who have no lifetime earnings; immigrate after age 25; die prior to retiring or becoming disabled; or become disabled prior to age 45.

Table 9. Sample Summary Statistics, PENSIM 1990 Cohort, Medians

	Full	By income quartile			
Workforce variables	sample	1	2	3	4
Years working full-time	29.4	14.1	27.9	31.8	34.8
Years working part-time	2.1	9.1	2.2	1.1	0.5
Steady earnings (annual, 2007 dollars)	46,122	16,820	34,950	60,777	126,380
Number of jobs over lifetime	5.0	5.0	5.0	5.0	5.0
Duration of longest job, years	17.2	13.4	16.9	18.3	19.5
Retirement age	63.0	62.0	63.0	63.0	64.0
Years eligible for DC pension	18.5	9.4	17.6	21.2	25.2

Source: GAO calculations of PENSIM simulation of 1990 cohort.

Cross-sectional results of the sample cohort also provide some insights into the model's assumptions, as well as some further insights into the relatively low projected sample replacement rates (see table 10). These statistics describe the working characteristics for each employed individual at a randomly determined age sometime between 22 and 62 in order to provide a snapshot of a "current" job for most of the sample.

Among those employed at the time of the survey, 61.8 percent had an employer who sponsors a DC plan. Of these workers with a plan offered, 94 percent were eligible to participate, and among those eligible 67 percent participated. Taking all of these percentages together, this means that at any one time only 38.9 percent of the working population actively participated in a DC plan in our projections. Even among these participants, only 56.9 percent reported making a contribution to the plan in the previous year, while 45.7 percent had an employer contribution. Median combined employer-employee contributions in the previous year were 6.2 percent of earnings in our simulation.

Table 10. Cross-Sectional Pension Characteristics of Sample

	Average	Median
Age at survey	42.1	42.1
Percent of sample employed	71.5	
Current job duration (years)	8.0	5.9
Job offers DC plan	61.8	
Among offered, percent eligible to participate	93.9	
Among eligible, percent participating	67.0	
Past year's employee contribution (percent of earnings)	4.3	3.9
Past year's employer contribution (percent of earnings)	3.1	0
Total contribution (percent of earnings)	7.4	6.2
Cumulative returns per year in plan (2007 dollars)	1,303	383
Cumulative returns in current plan (2007 dollars)	22,318	180
Among eligible, percent contributing in past year	56.9	
Among eligible, percent with employer contribution in past year	45.7	

Source: GAO calculations of PENSIM simulation of 1990 cohort.

Note: Results reflect one time snapshot of each member of the sample at a randomly determined age between 22 and 62.

Appendix II: Comparison of DC Plan Projections Based on PENSIM to Other Studies

Other studies have projected DC plan savings for workers saving over their entire working careers. These studies generally find higher projected replacement rates from DC plan savings than our simulations do.

However, each study makes different key assumptions, particularly about plan coverage, participation, and contributions.

A 2007 study by Patrick Purcell and Debra B. Whitman for the Congressional Research Service (CRS) simulates DC plan replacement rates based on earnings, contributions, and the rate of return on plan balances.[1] CRS projects savings for households that begin saving at age 25, 35, or 45. The study estimates 2004 earnings using the March 2005 CPS as starting wages, and assumes that households experience an annual wage growth rate of 1.1 percent. Households are randomly assigned a 6 percent, 8 percent, or 10 percent retirement plan contribution rate every year from their starting age until age 65. The study assumes households allocate 65 percent of their retirement account assets to Standard & Poor's 500 index of stocks from ages 25 to 34, 60 percent to stocks from ages 35 to 44, 55 percent to stocks from ages 45 to 54, and 50 percent to stocks from age 55 and above, with the remaining portfolio assets invested in AAA-rated corporate bonds. A Monte Carlo simulation based on historical returns on stocks and bonds determines annual rates of return. Replacement rates represent annuitized DC plan balances at age 65 divided by final 5-year average pay.

After running the simulations, CRS finds variation in replacement rates depending on rate of return, years of saving, and earning percentile. In the CRS "middle estimate," the unmarried householder that saves for 30 years, has annual household earnings in the 50th percentile, contributes 8 percent each year until retirement, and earns returns on contributions in the 50th percentile would have a 50 percent replacement rate (see table 11). The projected replacement rate jumps to 98 percent at 40 years of saving, and 22 percent at just 20 years of saving. Assuming a 6 percent annual contribution reduces projected replacement rates by about 10 to 30 percent. For example, an unmarried householder at the 50th percentile of annual earnings and the 50th percentile of returns saving for 40 years is projected to have a replacement rate of 72 percent at a 6 percent annual contribution (see table 12). All CRS estimates, however, exceed those we report in projections in this report, in part because CRS assumes constant participation in, and contributions to, a DC plan. In addition, CRS calculated annuity equivalents of accumulated DC balances based on current annuity prices; for younger workers retiring several decades into the future, we would expect the price of a given level of annuity income to be higher than today's levels because of longer life expectancies. This would lower the replacement rates for any projected lump sum.

Table 11. Retirement Savings and Income Replacement Rates for Unmarried Householders, Annual Total Contributions Equal to 8 Percent of Household Earnings and 50th Percentile of Returns (2004 Dollars)

	Age household begins saving	Annual household earnings percentile		
Baseline replacement rates (percent)		75th	50th	25th
	25	.91	.98	1.05
	35	.47	.50	.53
	45	.21	.22	.24

Source: Patrick Purcell, and Debra B. Whitman. "Retirement Savings: How Much Will Workers Have When They Retire?" Congressional Research Service, January 29, 2007.

Note: Replacement rates represent annuitized DC plan balances at age 65 divided by final 5-year average pay.

Table 12. Retirement Savings and Income Replacement Rates for Unmarried Householders, Annual Total Contributions Equal to 6 Percent of Household Earnings and 50th Percentile of Returns (2004 dollars)

	Age household begins saving	Annual household earnings percentile		
Baseline replacement rates (percent)		75th	50th	25th
	25	.67	.72	.77
	35	.35	.37	.40
	45	.16	.17	.18

Source: Purcell and Whitman, 2007.

Note: Replacement rates represent annuitized DC plan balances at age 65 divided by final 5-year average pay.

A 2005 study, by Sarah Holden of ICI and Jack VanDerhei of EBRI, simulates, as a baseline scenario, retirement savings at age 65 for a group in their 20s and 30s in the year 2000.2 The baseline assumes workers are continuously covered by a DC plan throughout their career, and that workers will continuously participate. However, the authors also run the model assuming this group will have participation rates similar to current rates by allowing workers to not be covered by, participate in, or contribute to a DC plan.[3] Their model also incorporates the possibility that a participant might cash out a DC plan balance upon leaving a job. Replacement rates are calculated by earnings quartile for participants retiring between 2035 and 2039 as the annuity value of age-65 plan balances divided by final 5-year average pay.

The EBRI/ICI baseline projections, starting with a sample of plan participants, show a median replacement rate of 51 percent for the lowest earnings quartile and 67 percent for the highest. (See table 13). The authors analyze the effect of other plan or behavioral assumptions. For example, replacement rates fall significantly when the projections relax the assumption of continuous ongoing eligibility for a 401(k) plan, although they remain higher than our projections, perhaps because the projections start with current participants and assume continuous employment. When the authors include nonparticipants and assume automatic enrollment with a 6 percent employee contribution and investment of assets in a life cycle fund, replacement rates rise significantly from projections without automatic enrollment. Although they project a larger effect on replacement rates resulting from automatic enrollment than our projections show, EBRI/ICI similarly shows a greater increase in savings for lower-income workers.

Table 13. Median Replacement Rates from DC Plan Balances for Workers Turning 65 between 2030 and 2039, by Income Quartile

Replacement rates				
Income quartile	Baseline, assuming continuous eligibility, participants only	Without continuous eligibility	With continuous eligibility, including non-participants	With continuous eligibility and automatic enrollment, including nonparticipants
1st	.51	.23	.23	.52
2nd	.54	.23	.33	.54
3rd	.59	.25	.43	.57
4th	.67	.28	.56	.63

Source: Sarah Holden and Jack VanDerhei. "The Influence of Automatic Enrollment, Catch-Up, and IRA Contributions on 401(k) Accumulations at Retirement." *Investment Company Institute Perspective*, vol. 11, No. 2, July 2005); co-published as EBRI *Issue Brief* No. 283 (Washington, D.C.: Jul. 2005).

Note: Replacement rates equal income generated from DC savings divided by final 5-year average salary.

A forthcoming study by Poterba, Venti, and Wise uses the Survey of Income and Program Participation (SIPP) to project DC plan balances at age 65.[4] In order to project participation, the authors assume that DC plan sponsorship will continue to grow, although more slowly than during recent decades.[5] They calculate participation by earnings deciles within 5- year age intervals. The authors assume that 60 percent of plan contributions are allocated to large capitalization equities, and 40 percent to corporate bonds, and assume an average nominal rate of return of 12 percent for equities and 6 percent for corporate bonds. In addition, the authors run a projection assuming the rate of return on equities is 300 basis points less than the historical rate. They determine a person's likelihood of DC plan participation based on age, cohort, and earnings, as well as the probability of cashing out an existing DC plan balance when someone leaves a job. The authors simulate earnings histories based on data from the Health and Retirement Study (HRS), and impute earnings for younger cohorts for which data are not available. They assume an annual combined employee-employer contribution rate of 10 percent for each year an individual participates, and do not account for increases in annual contributions or changes made to DC plans in the Pension Protection Act, such as a possible increase in participation by automatically enrolling employees.

Table 14. Mean Projected DC Plan Assets for Cohorts Retiring in 2000, 2010, 2020, 2030, and 2040, by Lifetime Earnings Deciles (in 2000 dollars)

Baseline retirement savings ($)			
	Lifetime earning decile		
Cohort	1st	5th	10th
2000	0	19,437	166,405
2010	158	28,367	343,137
2020	366	166,268	577,632
2030	1,372	272,135	895,179
2040	3,688	489,558	1,242,580

Source: James Poterba, Steven F. Venti and David A. Wise. "New Estimates of the Path of 401(k) Assets," forthcoming in J. Poterba, ed., Tax Policy and the Economy, vol. 22 (Chicago: University of Chicago Press, 2008).

The authors find retirement savings for individuals retiring by decade between 2000 and 2040 by lifetime earning deciles. For workers in the fifth earnings decile retiring in 2030 at age 65, the authors project a mean DC plan balance of $272,135 in 2000 dollars, and $895,179 for the highest earning decile (see table 14). Earners in the lowest and second deciles, however, project average balances of $1,372, and $21,917. The projected average DC plan assets for 2030 retirees fall to $179,540 for the fifth decile of earnings, $614,789 for the highest decile, and $810 for the lowest decile when the authors assume an annual rate of return 300 basis points below the historic rate of return (see table 15).

Table 15. Mean Projected DC Plan Assets for Cohorts Retiring in 2000, 2010, 2020, 2030, and 2040, Assuming Rate of Return on Equities is 300 Basis Points Less than Historic Rate, by Lifetime Earnings Deciles (in 2000 dollars)

Retirement savings (2000 dollars)			
	Lifetime earning decile		
Cohort	**1st**	**5th**	**10th**
2000	0	19,437	166,405
2010	147	75,555	315,294
2020	335	128,920	454,171
2030	810	179,540	614,789
2040	2,072	292,902	785,150

Source: Poterba, Venti, and Wise, forthcoming 2008.

Finally, a 2007 study by William Even and David Macpherson estimates replacement rate for those continuously enrolled in a DC plan between 36 and 65 years of age.[6] The authors simulate a sample using the SCF, and generate an age earnings profile for their sample using data on pension-covered workers in the 1989 SCF. The authors also use the SCF to generate annual contributions to DC plans, which are estimated using a person's earnings, age, education, gender, race, ethnicity, marital status, union coverage, and firm size. The authors also create an artificial sample for workers who are predicted to be eligible for a DC plan, but choose not to participate. Finally, the authors assume three different rates of return on pension contributions: a 3 percent rate of return based on historical returns on government bonds; a historic returns portfolio based on an account mix of 75 percent in stocks split between large and small capital equities, and 25 percent split between long term corporate bonds, long term government bonds, midterm government bonds, and Treasury bills; a 6.5 percent real rate of returns based on the average real rate of return on DC plans from 1985 to 1994 for plans with over 100 participants. In calculating annuity rates, the authors rely on mortality tables for group annuitants as opposed to the population as a whole, and do not include the charge the company makes for marketing and administrative expenses.

The authors find that replacement rates vary by income distribution.[7] For example, low-income workers who are continuously enrolled in a DC plan at the median replacement rate distribution are estimated to have a 30 percent replacement rate. (see table 16) The average replacement rate for such workers is 44 percent. Middle-income and high-income workers have median replacement rates 31 percent and 35 percent respectively. The authors' estimates are likely higher than ours because the authors assume continuous enrollment.

Table 16. Replacement Rates by Income

Income	Replacement rate
Low	.30
Middle	.31
High	.35

Source: William Even and David Macpherson. "Defined Contribution Plans and the Distribution of Pension Wealth." *Industrial Relations,* Vol. 46, Number 3. July, 2007.

End Notes

[1] Further, the Social Security normal retirement age for receiving full benefits has begun rising from age 65 until reaching age 67 starting in 2027, a fact that will reduce benefits, relative to current rules, for those retiring at a given age.

[2] The SCF is conducted every 3 years to provide detailed information on the balance sheet, pension, income, and other demographic characteristics of U.S. families. The 2004 survey is the most recently published survey. Data from the SCF are widely used by branches of the U.S. government and major economic research centers. Further detail about the SCF and GAO's analysis can be found in app. I.

[3] A typical "final average pay" plan might set annual benefits equal to 1.5 percent of the average of the employee's final 5 years of earnings multiplied by the employee's tenure at the firm in years.

[4] Beginning in 2006, plans were permitted to allow employees to designate some contributions to Roth 401(k) plans, which are not excluded from current income but allow for tax-free withdrawals in retirement. Economic Growth and Tax Relief Reconciliation Act of 2001, Pub. L. No. 107-16, § 617, 115 Stat. 38, 103-06 (codified at 26 U.S.C. § 402A).

[5] 26 U.S.C. § 72(t). The Internal Revenue Code (IRC) sets limits on annual contributions to DC plans by both employees and employers. 26 U.S.C. § 415(c). In 2007, an employee may make up to $15,500 in tax-deductible contributions into a DC plan, and employee and employer combined contributions cannot exceed $45,000. A worker age 50 or older may contribute an additional $5,000 in annual "catch-up" contributions. The IRC exempts distributions from DC plans from an additional 10 percent tax if taken for certain purposes. 26 U.S.C. § 72(t)(2). For example, if the employee becomes disabled, needs funds for medical purposes, or if the distribution is taken upon separation of service at age 55, the additional tax does not apply.

[6] This tax expenditure includes Keogh plans ($10 billion), 401(k) plans ($41 billion), employee stock ownership plans ($2 billion), and the saver's credit ($1 billion). Summing these figures does not take into account any interactions. In addition, the tax expenditure for DB plans measured $49 billion and for IRAs measured $4 billion.

[7] The saver's credit is a credit against federal income tax available to low-and middle-income taxpayers based on their qualified contributions to 401(k) and other retirement savings plans and to IRAs. 26 U.S.C. § 25B. The Pension Protection Act of 2006 made the saver's credit permanent and indexed qualifying taxable income levels for inflation. Pub. L. No. 109-280 §§ 812 and 833(a), 120 Stat. 997, 1003-04.

[8] About 87 percent of all 401(k) plans generally allow participants to choose how much to invest, within federal limits, and to select from a menu of diversified investment options selected by the employer sponsoring the plan, such as an assortment of mutual funds that include a mix of stocks, bonds, and money market investments.

[9] A DC plan sponsor may make an automatic distribution of a participant's account balance when the participant leaves a job if the balance does not exceed $5,000. However, if the balance exceeds $1,000, the sponsor must automatically roll this money over into a default IRA or keep the balances in the plan, unless the participant explicitly chooses otherwise. 26 U.S.C. § 401(a)(31).

[10] The Pension Benefit Guaranty Corporation (PBGC) guarantees the payment of most private sector DB pension benefits in the event of sponsor termination of an underfunded plan, up to certain limits. 29 U.S.C. §§ 1322 and 1322a. For plans terminating in 2007, PBGC pays a maximum of $4,125 per month for a single straight-life annuity to a 65-year-old retiree, with lower guarantees for younger retirees.

[11] See Craig Copeland, "Individual Account Retirement Plans: An Analysis of the 2004 Survey of Consumer Finances," Employee Benefit Research Institute *Issue Brief,* No. 293 (Washington, D.C.: May 2006).

[12] A typical employer match might, for example, equal 50 percent of employee contributions on the first 6 percent of deferred employee salary.

[13] Some employers sponsor cash balance plans, which have some characteristics of both DB and DC plans. While cash balance plans express accrued benefits in terms of a lump-sum balance, they are DB plans in which benefits are determined by formula. For more on cash balance plans, see GAO, *Private Pensions: Information on Cash Balance Pension Plans,* GAO-06-42 (Washington, D.C.: Nov. 3, 2005); *Cash Balance Plans: Implications for Retirement Income,* HEHS-00-207 (Washington, D.C.: Sept. 29, 2000); and *Private Pensions: Implications of Conversions to Cash Balance Plans,* HEHS-00-185 (Washington, D.C.: Sept. 29, 2000).

[14] Many factors affect how much a person will need: age at retirement, life expectancy, living expenses, health expenses, investment returns, inflation, and personal tolerance for risk. For summaries of this research through 2002 and 2003, see GAO, *Private Pensions: Improving*

Worker Coverage and Benefits, GAO-02-225 (Washington, D.C.: April 9, 2002), pp. 41-44; and Congressional Budget Office, *Baby Boomers' Retirement Prospects: An Overview*, November 2003.

[15] For an example of such calculations, see Alicia Munnell, Anthony Webb, and Luke Delorme; "Retirement at Risk: A New National Retirement Index," Center for Retirement Research, June 2006 available at http://www.crr.bc.edu. In this research, replacement rates are calculated for households with differing lifetime income levels. Lower-income households are found to need a higher replacement rate due to lower saving during working years while higher-income households need a lower replacement rate. Because higher-income households tend to save relatively more while working, once retired they will no longer need to save a relatively large fraction of income.

[16] Most studies have found that at least 50 percent of households are likely to have adequate retirement income, while at least 20 percent of households are likely not to have adequate income. Research findings differ on the remaining 30 percent of households.

[17] Data reported by the Social Security Administration (SSA) do not consider lump-sum withdrawals from retirement accounts, such as DC plans or IRAs, as income, and hence these statistics do not include non-annuitized savings.

[18] SSA defines a low earner as someone whose career average earnings are about 45 percent of the national average wage index (AWI), while a high earner has career average earnings of about 160 percent of AWI.

[19]These are sample estimates based on the 2004 SCF and are subject to sampling error. Most SCF percentage estimates have 95 percent confidence intervals between plus-or-minus 4 percentage points of the percentage itself. The majority of SCF estimates of medians and means have 95 percent confidence intervals within plus-or-minus 25 percent of the estimate itself. Exceptions to these rules are presented in appendix I. The SCF is designed to produce estimates for a subset of the household, referred to as the "primary economic unit." There are limitations in extending this to an individual or worker level of analysis. Additional details can also be found in app. I.

[20] The 95 percent confidence interval for this estimate is from $27,594 to $72,406. While the range is broad, this statistic still effectively illustrates the limited DC savings of those currently near retirement age.

[21] Employees are to be eligible for pension plans once they reach one year of service or the age of 21. In order to fulfill the year of service requirement, employees must have worked for the employer for 12 months and fulfilled 1,000 hours of service." 26 U.S.C. §§ 401(a)(3), 410(a)(1)(A) and (3)(A).

[22] This participation figure includes all retirement plans, including both DB and DC plans. Because employees covered by DB plans are by definition, almost universally participants, the participation rate for DC plans is below the 84 percent figure.

[23] Retirement plans rolled over from a former employer could have originally been either DC or DB plans. Also, any retirement plans from a former employer that were converted into an annuity would not be captured in these "total balance" statistics.

[24] We calculated this yearly income, as an annuity equivalent using the Thrift Savings Plan calculator (http://calc.tsp.gov), assuming an interest rate of 5.25 percent, single life benefits beginning at age 65, no joint survivor benefits, and level payments. The 95 percent confidence interval for this annuity estimate is from $2,431 to $6,377 per year for life.

[25] 26 U.S.C. §§ 401(a) and 408(d).

[26] 26 U.S.C. § 72(t). See footnote 5 above for distributions that do not trigger a 10 percent early-withdrawal additional tax.

[27] Households included in this analysis of lump-sum distributions are restricted to those where the head of household is under age 59 in order to approximate those that would be subject to penalties for cashing out the retirement funds. Percentages do not add up to 100 percent because of rounding.

[28] These rollover and cash-out figures look at all cash settlements from past jobs. The SCF does not specify the original account type, so the analysis includes all retirement plans or pensions that were converted into a lump-sum distribution or settlement.

[29] See "Lump-Sum Distributions," EBRI *Notes*, vol. 26, No. 12 (Washington, D.C.: Dec. 2005).

[30] Profit Sharing/401(k) Council of America. "49th Annual Survey: PSCA's Annual Survey of Profit Sharing and 401(k) Plans Reflecting the 2005 Plan Experience" (Chicago, Ill.: 2006).

[31] Jack VanDerhei, Sarah Holden, Craig Copeland, and Luis Alonso, "401(k) Plan Asset Allocation, Account Balances, and Loan Activity in 2006." EBRI, *Issue Brief,* No. 308 (Washington, D.C.: Aug. 2007).

[32] See GAO, *401(k) Pension Plans: Loan Provisions Enhance Participation but May Affect Income Security for Some,* GAO/HEHS-98-5 (Washington, D.C.; Oct. 1, 1997).

[33] Since some older workers may have reduced their hours or are both retired and working, they may be earning less than they had been through most of their working life. Household wealth can more accurately reflect their financial situation than income can.

[34] The 95 percent confidence interval for this estimate of total DC balances of workers aged 60-64 at or below the median level of wealth is from $3,234 to $32,766. The 95 percent confidence intervals for these annuity estimates would be from $24 to $240 per month or from $285 to $2,883 per year.

[35] Replacement rates equal the annuity value of DC plan balances divided by a "steady earnings" index. This index reflects career earnings, calibrated to the Social Security Administration's age-65 average wage index (AWI). See app. I for further details about these calculations.

[36] We computed these results using the PENSIM simulation model, which creates a hypothetical birth cohort and models the cohort's lives from birth to death, including all life events such as marriages, births, education and job decisions, pension coverage and behavior, and retirement. Our simulations and results exclude any DB and Social Security benefits and calculate benefits from DC plans only. Annuity amounts assume full annuitization of DC balances at retirement for a single lifetime annuity not indexed to inflation. See app. I for detailed information about the projections and input assumptions used to produce the results presented in this section.

[37] Other studies that do similar DC plan balance projections that focus primarily on workers with continuous plan coverage generally find higher savings levels and replacement rates than we report in this section. We discuss these studies in more detail in app. II.

[38] All annuity equivalents for accumulated DC savings presented in this section are not indexed to inflation, and hence would lose purchasing power over time.

[39] This 2.9 percent annual return on assets represents a projected rate of return on U.S. Treasury bonds. While stocks have had greater long-term historical average returns, annual stock returns also exhibit more variance than Treasury bonds, and therefore we model DC plan projections under different scenarios. For more discussion of the appropriate rate to use in projections, see app. I.

[40] We recalculate income quartiles for the sub-samples, and thus the income cut-offs for each quartile differ from those in the full-sample baseline.

[41] While this scenario eliminates waiting periods for eligibility and participation among workers of firms that sponsor plans, it does not necessarily imply that workers are making a contribution to a plan each period, nor does it affect the likelihood that a firm will offer a

DC plan. PENSIM determines periodic contribution levels among participants based on plan features and worker characteristics. See app. I.

[42] In our baseline scenario, workers cash out account balances 36 percent of the time when leaving a job.

[43] The baseline projections assume that annual contribution limits continue to rise in the future from 2007 limits of $15,500 for employee contributions and $45,000 for combined employer-employee contributions.

[44] We would expect the effect on annuity income to exceed that on replacement rates because working longer may also raise our measure of career earnings that we use in the denominator of the replacement rate calculation.

[45] Pub. L. No. 109-280, § 902, 120 Stat. 780, 1033-39.

[46] Jodi DiCenzo, "Behavioral Finance and Retirement Plan Contributions: How Participants Behave, and Prescriptive Solutions," EBRI *Issue Brief* No. 301 (Washington, D.C.: Jan. 2007).

[47] See William G. Gale, J. Mark Iwry, and Peter R. Orszag, "The Automatic 401(k): A Simple Way to Strengthen Retirement Savings," The Retirement Security Project, No. 2005-1 (Washington, D.C.: Mar. 2005); and William G. Gale, J. Mark Iwry, and Spencer Walters, "Retirement Saving for Middle- and Lower-Income Households: The Pension Protection Act of 2006 and the Unfinished Agenda," The Retirement Security Project, No. 2007-1 (Washington, D.C.: 2007).

[48] Brigitte C. Madrian and Dennis F. Shea. "The Power of Suggestion: Inertia in 401(k) Participation and Savings Behavior." *The Quarterly Journal of Economics*, vol. 116, Issue 4 (Nov. 2001). The authors compare participation rates for those hired at a large firm in the health-care and insurance industry, before automatic enrollment (with 1 year of service required to be eligible), and those hired after automatic enrollment (with immediate eligibility for all employees, and all newly hired employees auto-enrolled).

[49] Our simulation projections show that immediate plan eligibility and participation would increase the average annuity equivalent of retirement savings for workers by almost 40 percent, with replacement rates for lowest-income quartile workers' savings growing from 10.3 percent in our baseline model to 25.4 percent. This simulation undoubtedly overstates the effect of auto enrollment provisions under PPA; since employers are not compelled to offer auto enrollment, it may apply only to new employees, and it is difficult to predict the effect of auto enrollment on employer's willingness to sponsor a plan.

[50] See Rev. Rul. 98-30 and 1998-1 C.B. 1273. In 2000, additional rulings provided that various automatic plan features were permissible, including automatic enrollment of both newly hired employees and nonenrolled incumbent employees, and automatic enrollment in 403(b) and 457, as well as in 401(k), plans, and allowed automatic investment. See Rev. Rul. 2000-8, 2000-1 C.B. 617, Rev. Rul. 2000-35, 2000-2 C.B. 138; Rev. Rul. 2000-33, and 2000-1 C.B. 142. However, there was no certainty regarding the extent to which employers would face greater exposure to liability for losses to employee accounts due to default investment choices in automatic enrollment plans. The PPA addressed this uncertainty by directing the Department of Labor to provide a measure of additional protection to plan fiduciaries that use certain kinds of default investments, PPA § 624, 120 Stat. 980 and 72 Fed. Reg. 60,452 (Oct. 24, 2007), and the Department recently issued final regulations providing such protection.

[51] See Profit Sharing/401(k) Council of America. "48th Annual Survey of Profit Sharing and 401(k) Plans Reflecting 2004 Plan Experience" (Chicago, Ill.: 2005); and "49th Annual

Survey: PSCA's Annual Survey of Profit Sharing and 401(k) Plans Reflecting the 2005 Plan Experience" (Chicago, Ill.: 2006, August 2007).

[52] For instance, PPA specified that the Employee Retirement Income Security Act of 1974 (ERISA) pre-empted state payroll or anti-garnishment laws that might be interpreted to prohibit automatic deferral of employees pay. PPA § 902(f), 120 Stat. 1039.

[53] One recent study suggests the absence of an employer match in an automatic-enrollment 401(k) scheme has little impact on participation. Thus, the authors suggest that a non-matching automatic-enrollment type scheme, such as an automatic IRA, could have a significant impact on participation and savings. This study finds that the absence of an employer match in an automatic 401(k) plan only modestly decreases participation, implying that an automatic payroll deposit plan such as an IRA could be successful in increasing participation even without an employer match. (John Beshears et al. "The Impact of Employer Matching on Savings Plan Participation Under Automatic Enrollment." National Bureau of Economic Research, Working Paper 13352, August 2007.)

[54] The Department of Labor's final regulation regarding default contributions, which is to take effect December 24, 2007, specifies what constitutes a "qualified default investment alternative," which includes life cycle funds, balanced funds, and managed accounts, as well as grandfathered and short-term principal preservation funds. 72 Fed. Reg. 60,470-80.

[55] PPA specifies that each employee will be given ninety days to withdraw from the automatic enrollment plan and distributions taken within this time period will be penalty free. PPA § 902, 120 Stat. 780, 1033-39.

[56] Several states have proposed or have been exploring State-Ks, including Washington, Maryland, Michigan, and Vermont. For additional information on the State-K concept, see J. Mark Iwry, "State-K: A Strategy for Using State-Assisted Saving to Expand Private Pension Coverage." Supplemental Written Testimony before the Sub-Committee on Long-Term Growth and Debt Reduction of the Committee on Finance, US Senate. Jun. 29, 2006; and J. Mark Iwry, "Growing Private Pensions: A Supporting Role for the States," BNA Tax Management *Compensation Planning Journal,* vol. 34, no. 12 (Washington, D.C.: Dec. 1, 2006).

[57] H.B. 1414, 423[d] Gen. Assem., Reg. Sess. (Md. 2006).

[58] See J. Mark Iwry and David C. John, Testimony Before the Subcommittee on Health, Employment, Labor, and Pensions of the House Education and Labor Committee (Nov. 8, 2007) and "Pursuing Universal Retirement Security Through Automatic IRAs," Retirement Security Project, No. 2007-2 (Washington, D.C.: 2007). The automatic IRA proposal differs from existing employment-based IRAs, such as the SEP-IRA and SIMPLE IRAs, which require employer contributions. In the SEP, small business employees 21 and over who have worked at least 3 of the past 5 years for the employer, and who earn at least $450 qualify. 26 U.S.C. § 408(k). Contributions cannot discriminate in favor of highly compensated employees. SIMPLE plans can be adopted by employers who have no more than 100 employees who earned at least $5,000 the previous year. 26 U.S.C. § 408(p). In 2007, employee contributions to a SIMPLE IRA were limited to $10,500, including elective deferrals and employer deferrals. Employers must either match employee contributions dollar for dollar up to 3 percent of pay, with the option of contributing as little as 1 percent of pay for 2 out of 5 years, or make automatic non-elective contributions to employee accounts of 2 percent of pay. In addition, employers can also allow employees to make direct payroll contributions to IRAs without making matching contributions to the IRA. 26 U.S.C. § 408(q).

[59]Automatic IRA Act of 2007, S. 1141, 110th Congress (as introduced April 18, 2007) and H.R. 2167, 110th Congress (as introduced May 3, 2007).

[60] See David M. Walker, "Fiscal and Retirement Challenges." Presentation to the UJA Foundation of New York, September 2007, and Burman, Leanord E, William G. Gale and Peter R. Orszag. "The Administration's Savings Proposals: Preliminary Analysis." *Tax Analysts*, 2003.

[61] See GAO, *Social Security: Evaluating Reform Proposals.* GAO/AIMD/HEHS-00-29 (Washington, D.C.; Nov. 4, 1999). See also U.S. Department of the Treasury, General Explanations of the Administration's Fiscal Year 2001 Revenue Proposals (Feb. 2000), pages 49-52.

[62] See William G. Gale, J. Mark Iwry, and Peter R. Orszag, "The Saver's Credit: Issues and Options," (Washington, D.C.: May 3, 2004). One field experiment examined savings behavior for tax filers who were given the opportunity to open and contribute to an account, including an IRA, at the time of tax filing. Some of these filers were offered a match with a structure similar to the saver's credit that directly deposited funds into the account for the filers. Before the experiment, about 2 percent of all filers opened such an account, and average contributions for all taxpayers who opened an account were about $382. During the experiment, about 3 percent of those not offered a match opened an account and contributed an average of $765, about 8 percent of those offered a 20 percent match opened an account and contributed an average of $1,102, and about 14 percent of those offered the 50 percent match opened an account and contributed and average of $1,108. See Esther Duflo et al. "Saving Incentives for Low- and Middle-Income Families: Evidence from a Field Experiment with H&R Block." National Bureau of Economic Research, Working Paper 11680. Sept. 2005.

[63] See William G. Gale, J. Mark Iwry, and Peter Orszag. "Improving Tax Incentives for Low-Income Savers: The Saver's Credit." Urban Institute, Discussion Paper No. 22, page 13, and footnote 43 (Washington, D.C.: Jun. 2005).

End Notes for Appendix I

[1] Other estimates would include estimated means, medians, or projected annuities based on an estimated median account balance.

[2] Additional information and details about this technique are available from the Federal Reserve Board, http://www.federalreserve.gov/pubs/oss/oss2/about.html.

[3] Comparison data sets are the Survey of Income and Program Participation, the Current Population Survey, and the Department of Labor Form 5500 series. See Geoffrey Sanzenbacher; "Estimating Pension Coverage Using Different Data Sets," Center for Retirement Research, August 2006, for additional discussion on this topic.

[4] For more information on PSG microsimulation models, see http://www.polsim.com. For more details on PENSIM, see Martin Holmer, Asa Janney, and Bob Cohen, *PENSIM Overview*, available from http://www.polsim.com/overview.pdf.

[5] While these models use sample data, our report, like others using these models, does not address the issue of sampling errors. The results of the analysis reflect outcomes for individuals in the simulated populations and do not attempt to estimate outcomes for an actual population.

[6] The difference between the return on equities and Treasury bonds represents the compensation that individuals require for the higher risk of holding equities. Since our projections do not stochastically model stock returns, assuming a rate of return on assets equal to the historical return on stocks does not capture the risks associated with stock returns; we therefore also model DC savings under a scenario in which all assets return the government bond rate of return. For more discussion of the appropriate rate to use in projections, see "Analysis of H.R. 3304, Growing Real Ownership for Workers Act of 2005," Congressional Budget Office, Sept. 13, 2005, pp. 63-5.

[7] We classify as retired those workers who become disabled after age 62. We do not classify as disabled those workers who recover from a disability prior to age 62.

[8] We drop cohort members who die before retiring because we assume annuitizaton at retirement, but someone who dies before retiring would never annuitize his DC savings. We apply the other conditions because such cohort members are likely to have fewer years in the workforce to accumulate DC plan savings.

[9] The income quartile sub-samples used in this report are based on "steady earnings."

[10] See discussion of definition of "steady" earnings above.

End Notes for Appendix II

[1] Patrick Purcell and Debra B. Whitman. "Retirement Savings: How Much Will Workers Have When They Retire?" Congressional Research Service, January 29, 2007.

[2] Sarah Holden and Jack VanDerhei. "The Influence of Automatic Enrollment, Catch-Up, and IRA Contributions on 401(k) Accumulations at Retirement." *Investment Company Institute Perspective*, vol. 11, No. 2. (Washington, D.C.: Jul. 2005); co-published as EBRI *Issue Brief* No. 283 (Washington, D.C.: Jul. 2005).

[3] Because the EBRI/ICI database does not include information for nonparticipants, the authors generate nonparticipants using their model.

[4] James Poterba, Steven F. Venti and David A. Wise. "New Estimates of the Path of 401(k) Assets," forthcoming in J. Poterba, ed., *Tax Policy and the Economy,* vol. 22 (Chicago: University of Chicago Press, 2008).

[5] We ran a simulation in PENSIM assuming that all future pension plans are DC plans. Under this extreme scenario, we find average projected replacement rates from DC plan savings of 24.2 percent for a 1990 cohort. Lowest-income quartile replacement rates measured 11.5 percent, while highest-quartile replacement rates were 36.4 percent.

[6] William Even and David Macpherson. "Defined Contribution Plans and the Distribution of Pension Wealth." *Industrial Relations*, vol. 46, Number 3. July, 2007.

[7] The authors define a low group to have simulated earnings at age 65 of approximately $48,000 or less; the top third has income of approximately $70,000 or more.

INDEX

D

E

F

G

H

I

J

L

M

N

O

P

Q

R

S

T

U

V

W